EVERYTHING'S WRONT
Election Edition

Andrew Smith

Copyright © 2014, 2015, 2016 Andrew Smith
All rights reserved.
ISBN-13:
9780692730263 (PRIME PRODS PRESS)

ISBN-10:
0692730265
"The Swoosh," "Alternative 'Oscar' Montages," "Well, Hello, Barbie,"
"New Marijuana-Related Products, and "Bill Clinton's Pet Projects As
First Hubby" previously appeared in *Vanity Fair* in edited form.

Prime Prods Press: New York, NY
knatural@aol.com
www.andrewasmith.com
primeprodspress@aol.com
www.everythingswront.com

Dedicated to

Whoever actually *bought* this book instead of making me give you one free. You know who you are. Thanks.

CONTENTS

Preface ix

Body Man 1
Books Just For You To Put On Your Shelf That You
    Won't Find Anywhere Else 7
Challahdays 15
Discarded Chris Christie Campaign Slogans. 19
DOGTV. 22
First Lines Of The Eulogy For Arch West—
    The Inventor Of Doritos 26
Drone Delivery 28
Glitches In My Program, Or Something's Wront 36
Horoscope 41

Horse Drawn Out	49
LGBTWHA?	56
Madoff Madness	60
Masterpieces Of Self-Publishing	81
Uncoupling The Conscious	87
Immediate Military Changes Now That "Don't Ask/Don't Tell" Has Been Repealed	92
Individuals On My Government-Shutdown Furlough List	95
My Pot Not So Lucky	98
Oh, Mama!	105
Osama Bin Laden's Diary	111
Selfies	116
Don't Touch That Throat, My Friend	120
Suicide Bombing 101	124
Trump Campaign Bumper Stickers	130
Watchful What?	135
Anthony Weiner's Concession Speech	138
Our Wacky, Nutty President	141
Indications That Your Gynecologist Might Be Secretly Filming You	146
The Most Insensitive Man In The World	149
In Repose	152
From Eagle Scouts To Fabulous Scouts	162
Questionable Questions For The Republican Debates	168
The Swoosh	171
Table Of Contents For The New *Playboy* Magazine	175

If Every NFL Franchise Supported The Washington
    Redskins By Making Their Own Mascot Just As
    Distasteful And Politically Incorrect 179
ISIS Decides To Set Up A Caliphate At The
    North Pole Instead Of In The Middle East 182
The Latest In Summer Jobs For Sub-Millennials..... 186
New Breakup Lines For This Year's Summer
    Romances..................................... 190
2016 Presidential Campaign Nursery Rhymes....... 193
Powerball Winners Determined Not To Change
    Their Lives................................... 196
Well, Hello, Barbie............................... 200
My Psychiatrist Plays The Piano, Too 202
All Gender 205
Write What You Emoji 211
Memories Of The El Niño Winter Of Global
    Warming 216
A Statement From Charlie Sheen's Penis 219
Overheard At The St. Patrick's Day Parade 222
How You Know You Were Born Before 1996 224
Alternative Academy Awards Tribute Montages 226
My Dictionary By Donald Trump 230
New Marijuana-Related Products 235
If Marijuana Had Been Legal In The '60S
    And '70S...................................... 238
President Donald J. Trump—The First 100 Days..... 240
If Political-Campaign Sloganeers Wrote Headlines
    For E.D. Medication Ads....................... 247

Oscar Acceptance-Speech Mistakes 251
Unusual Film Credits............................ 253
Indications That Your Valentine Hates You 255
Stephen Hawking's Pickup Lines 257
"October Surprises" We Kinda Saw Coming 259
Ten Jokes Using The Comic Trope Of The Japanese
    Mispronunciation Of The Word *Erection* 263
"My Fair Marty" 265
Scamilton—The Musical 267
Weird Disorders In The Zoo Infirmary 270
Rules To Live By................................ 272
Dating Tips For Newly Divorced Men.............. 275
Bill Clinton's Pet Projects As "First Hubby" 279
More Donald Trump Products 284

PREFACE

Prefaces are bullshit, and this one is no exception. But I thought I should explain why *Everything's Wront* contains *Something's Wront* in its entirety—although I *did* actually update, edit, and punch up at least *some* of *Something's* pieces. But the main reason I included all of it is because I figured no one read *Something's Wront* anyway. So it's not like, "If you loved that, you'll love this." It's more like, "Look at all the shit I've written since Joy Behar fired me from *The View*." So if you're in a hurry, you can start with number 28 and go on from there. That's more than half the book of totally new stuff. That's worth the price right there. And even if you were nice enough to buy *Something's Wront,* I know you *still* didn't actually read it, so now's your chance. Everything in *Everything* is about the length of a decent trip to the toilet, so there's no excuse. It's not exactly *War and Peace*, for crissakes.

—Andrew Smith

BODY MAN

A body man accompanies the politician or candidate virtually everywhere, often arranging lodging, transportation, or meals and providing companionship, snacks, a cell phone, and any other necessary assistance.

—Wikipedia

Never thought I'd end up a body man, but here I am. It's a good job. Steady. Like, no one bothers you. That's *your* job. *You* do the botherin'. "Wait, lemme get that," I say about twenty times a day. It could be a thread, or worse, the guy mighta sat in somethin'. That's when I think, *I really shoulda gone to business school.* Maybe next year. Right now I'm lookin' at all these telltale sweat beads gatherin' on his upper lip. But I'm cool about it. I don't make no overt move. I don't do that. What I do is go up to the guy real close—*too* close unless you're the body man, if you know what I mean. *Real* close, and I look him right in the eye and hand him a handkerchief—linen, hemmed, no bleach, just the way he likes 'em. Then he gets the idea and appreciates I did it so nobody could see it. That's my job. Early warning system. NORAD with a handkerchief. I got eyes that penetrate every situation. Then he takes the handkerchief, pats down his upper lip, and hands it back to me. I take it like it was mine. I don't care. We're like brothers. Same cooties. Mission accomplished. Seal Team 6 got nothing on me. I know what that's all about. Service to a higher cause, and invisibility. Boom! I'm outta there, and nobody ever noticed me even though I was in plain sight. That's my job.

The governor really needs *two* body men. It's a big job in more ways than one, and I know what you're thinkin'. It's not just the size of the guy; he's a big personality—like Donald Trump if Trump were a nice guy. Trump has a body man. He has to. I can spot the signs. He probably has one who does nothin' but hair, but you never see him. *Never.* The governor's hair is easy. Bim, boom—over and out. But Trump has other issues. C'mon, get serious. Like he's a germ freak in public life. A body man's worst nightmare. In cases like that, the *body man* needs a body man because the guy isn't too sure about *you*, either. For all I know, Trump's got *three* body men. One just to take care of the other two so the guy doesn't get all freaked out over germs on his *number one* body man. Hey, think about that. A body man's body man. What's *that* all about?

Anyway, the governor's a great guy. I'd like to think I'm his friend, but I know I'm not. *Food* is this guy's friend. I've seen the look on his face when he gets near a buffet. If it was between me and a rack of lamb, I'd lose. Big-time. I know that. When you're a body man, you know your place in the scheme of things. The guy has food issues. That's pretty obvious. My job is to make sure those food issues don't spill over into a legislative session in Trenton—or worse, onto his tie. Or, maybe, the food thing is reflected in statements at a town meetin' that could prove embarrassin' to the guy and undermine his effectiveness as the elected leader of the Garden State. But what's good for the governor ain't always good for New Jersey. Sometimes I'm the only thing between him and a tiramisu during negotiations with the teachers union. But it ain't gonna happen when I'm around. That's what I get paid for. No crumbs, no smear, no dollop, no nothin' on the guy's fat face when he's doin' state business. You will *never* see him wipe his mouth with the back of his hand when he's raisin' tolls or chewin' out some caller on a radio show. I've had people say to me, "When *does* he eat?" That's how good I am as a body man.

Even when the guy had his lap-band surgery, he was real cool about it. No big deal. Coulda been just a couple of traffic cones across his duodenum for all anybody knew. Next thing you know, the job is done. Just like that. "Time for some traffic problems in the large intestines," the surgeon probably said. Everybody's a comedian.

But don't get me wrong. The governor's a big guy. I mean, a *big guy*. That's how I got the job. I used to be a crane operator at a container facility in Elizabeth. I was handpicked when they needed someone who could handle a guy like that after he became a candidate, and not just a prosecutor putting people away. But don't start with the "Beep, beep, beep" jokes every time the governor backs up. We've heard all that.

But the guy *could* use some lights back there. I feel like I'm workin' on a freakin' national monument over here. I'm handlin' undershorts as big as the Hoover Dam. There's enough leather in one of his belts to put shoes on a family of five. I wish my apartment was as big as the seat of his trousers. I'd be livin' in a floor-through. I always carry five shirts for the guy. He likes to sweat. I don't want to say "like a pig." That's disrespectful. Let's just say you could corner the bacon market with an option on this guy's belly. Anyway, the guy's collar size starts with a "2." OK? He has a neck that's measured in furlongs, not inches. Horses could run around it at Monmouth. Bam!

I say all this so you get an idea of what I'm up against as the governor's body man. I should wear a Smokey the Bear hat, only that would give me away. Sometimes it's more like bein' in the high-risk catering business than anything else. The man likes to eat. Lemme tell you somethin'. The most dangerous spot in America is standin' between him and lunch. Once I brought him a beautiful Black Forest ham and Swiss with lettuce, tomato, and mustard on seven-grain (he only eats rye on the "trail" for the Jewish vote). The guy bit right through the wax paper like a horse. Didn't even look at the sandwich itself until it was half-eaten. Then he says to me, "Where's the pickle?" and I say, "In your stomach, Governor, all nicely wrapped the way it came." I've seen him eat the panties off a lamb chop like he was Roman Polanski or somethin'. That's when I turn away out of respect.

My main job is to make sure none of the food stays on the governor after he's finished. That would be curtains for me as a body man, and for him as a serious presidential hopeful and governor of a swing state. Nobody knows this, but sometimes the guy's chin looks like a landfill. See? Nobody knows that because I take care of it for him. I have a special "wet one" that's just for his chin, and some carbon tetrachloride wipes for his tie and lapels. City Harvest should make a stop there.

Look, I'm the governor's body man, and even *I* don't know how he got that fat. He was that way long before me. They should call him Governor Crisco, if you ask me. Let's put it this way. He didn't get that way from just breathin'. It's called *food*, dummy. Craft services got nothin' on me. A disposal is anorexic compared to what goes down *this guy's* throat. He never met *nothin'* edible he didn't like, includin' a couple of things hitherto known as *inedible*, if you know what I mean. Don't press me on this, but if he was a dog, you'd have to take him to the vet to get an operation to remove some of those things, *pronto.*

Sometimes I'm a little jealous of the body men who travel with just a comb and a lint roller. Me? I'm like the guy who had to do cleanup after the loaves and fishes. He's a walkin' one-man Puerto Rican Day Parade. Every time he kisses a baby, I think he's gonna *swallow* it. Now, there's a vote getter. Takin' a bite outta an infant. Jeez! Anyway, it's pretty steady work, so that's a good thing. And who knows? Maybe the guy goes all the way. The next thing you know, I'm doing body work in the White House. But them state dinners there could be a nightmare. Maybe I should go on a diet myself first.

BOOKS JUST FOR YOU TO PUT ON YOUR SHELF THAT YOU WON'T FIND ANYWHERE ELSE

Condoms and Condominiums by Rebecca Rassmusen
A young couple overpays for a co-op, only to learn that the building houses not one but thirty brothels. Board meetings are fun, and the husband insists on serving.

Beat Me Silly by Fortunate [pseud.]
No comma needed in this S&M romp about a middle-aged spinster who rents out her toolshed to a fellow gardener who has more than mulch on his mind.

Angels on the Head of a Pin by Moira Finkle
In this fictional memoir, a coven of suburban housewives bands together to make a quilt that magically turns anyone who sews it fertile again. Recipes included.

Vlad the Impaler: A Historical Love Story by Jonathan Bleck
Misunderstood for centuries, "Vladdie" time-travels back to the period leading up to all that impaling nastiness in order to charm the father of the historian who will, eventually, vilify him into deciding to remain a virgin.

M-M-M-My S-S-S-Story by Henry McWilliams
A lifelong stutterer, McWilliams relates, in excruciating verisimilitude, his struggle to be fluent. Written as a transcript of the author's real-time testimony, *M-M-M-My S-S-S-Story* lets the reader experience firsthand the horrors of stuttering.

Cheezy by Mildred Horner (ages 2–8)
Enjoy a delightful romp with Cheezy, who just wants to be one of the cheeses. Ever since he was a small curd, Cheezy wanted to fit in, but the constantly arrogant Swiss, the pushy Jack, and the very snooty Gouda won't let him. Even the Laughing Cow makes fun of him. Then he ages, becomes pungent and runny, and proves that cheeses come in all shapes, sizes, and textures.

Bang, You're Dead by Major General Thomas "Pappy" Himmelstein
A homoerotic account of the Invasion of Grenada by the commander who led the troops in the first wave. General Himmelstein asks the question, "Can you fight a war with your shirt off?"

I, Poultry Hauler by Herman Danziger
Few people realize what it takes to get a chicken to market. The author has spent his life as a driver for one of the biggest poultry producers in America, and he doesn't mince words when it comes to this "rooster's-eye view" of the "last ride."

Aliens Who Love Too Much by Celeste Norman
In a delightful twist of standard sci-fi fare, highly intelligent creatures from outer space mistakenly land in Mexico instead of the United States. Their first order of business then becomes getting across the border without proper documentation. They wrongly assumed they would be welcomed.

How to Sweat by Link Millington
A workout book for shut-ins who find it hard to stay active or get to a gym. Coach Millington takes you through a series of bone-crushing exercises using household appliances and everyday objects.

Catch Me, Catch Me by Virginia Decker
As an online dating coach, Ms. Decker has coached tens of thousands of women in their search for lasting love on the Internet. Here, she turns her expertise to getting the "purchase order" (as she puts it) once you've met face-to-face. According to Decker, "Sales are always about the sizzle" whether it's used cars or your heart.

Tic-Tac-Toe Revealed by J. J. Brown
For the first time, the insidious message behind this innocuous game is brought to light by a mathematician who has spent his life delving into tic-tac-toe's mysteries. You'll learn how it's not just Xs and Os.

I Punch for a Living by Vivian Salter
A female conductor on Metro North has an affair with a divorced commuter. But will their tryst last longer than the ten-trip senior/disabled ticket he purchased under false pretenses? On top of that, he insists she wear the uniform for their assignations.

Life, the First Conspiracy by Aristotle Higgins
Everyone thinks they know about "life." We've all experienced it. But did you know it's also a carefully constructed conspiracy? Higgins uncovers, for the first time, the "big lie" that has been perpetrated for centuries. Life, it turns out, isn't all it's cracked up to be.

Is God OK? by Muriel Tatlor
God gets sick. It happens. And what always makes Him feel better? The chicken soup of mankind, lovingly prepared and piping hot. Muriel Tatlor's engaging account of what we can do to please God. It's more than mindless obedience. It's "liquid love."

Hidden Avatars of Homosexuality by Phillippe
Is the chaise longue just a gay chair? Homosexuality is everywhere in this whimsical catalog of objects and their true sexual identity. Phillippe is the pseudonym of an internationally famous designer who prefers to remain closeted for reasons of political reprisal and client confidentiality.

A Life without Clothes by Claire and Jim Golfinopoulos
This daring couple gave up all trappings of modern life for a full year of nudity, and wrote about it in this amusing—but sometimes sad—account of what it's like to be Adam and Eve in modern-day America. It's life after the apple but before pants.

Crazy 101 by Sammy Klemperer
A young man is diagnosed with severe paranoid schizophrenia as well as bipolar and borderline disorders but decides to go to Yale anyway rather than be institutionalized. What he finds out is that not all the inmates are in the asylum. Some of them are poli-sci majors and graduating with honors.

Real Jesus by Rev. Francis L. Menkin
Did Jesus wear shoes when he walked on water, or did he go barefoot just in case? Father Menkin, a priest in his own right, explores a side of Our Savior rarely seen or talked about. *Real Jesus* is real interesting.

A Pet in Every Pot by Martin Salko
What better way to honor Fluffy than by serving her up well roasted for Sunday dinner? Salko, who has been in the livestock business for more than forty years, feels that household pets should come from the ranks of farm animals including, but not limited to, pigs, sheep, cows, and chickens that are routinely slaughtered without ever feeling the love that one can have for a pet.

Striving for Mediocrity by Anthony Edgewood
A lifelong quest to be unremarkable is the subject of Anthony Edgewood's latest treatise on "the brilliance of the normal." Here, Edgewood outlines steps that you can take each day to be "nothing special," which, we learn, is special enough in its own way.

The Rotary-Dial Murders by Oliver Rankin
A serial killer is terrorizing the elderly of Fairdale, Indiana. Are the murders connected, or are they just random acts of elder abuse? It takes a regular housewife with a new manicure to discover the rotary phone as an overlooked clue that leads to the killer.

Sex and the Single Cell by Dr. Seymour Katz
Amoebas and other single-cell creatures have a sex life that defies all convention and norms of higher life forms. This highly readable treatise comes with revealing pictures of microscopic hijinks and molecular orgies.

Murder at the Carnegie Deli by Kurt Bledsoe
Someone is killing the waiters at the famous delicatessen. The owners turn to famed Jewish sleuth Sherlock Holmestein, himself a patron, to find the murderer. Is it Nazis? The Health Department? A lousy tipper? Holmestein quickly finds the culprit but is strangely ambivalent about solving the case.

Whaddja Eat? by Umberto Goetz
Every meal eaten by the author since 1962 has been recorded in dazzling detail. Relive the '60s and the partying '80s in this gastronomically compelling narrative of breakfasts, lunches, dinners, and midnight snacks. It's January 9, 1981. Do you know what *you* ate?

P Is for Poetry by Esther Coleman
Twenty-six one-letter poems that will break your heart and heal your soul.

Live Almost Forever! by Salvador Jenks, PhD
It's all about getting close to the speed of light. Professor Jenks feels that the earth is what's killing us. If we could

only get into outer space and approach the speed of light, we could extend our lives to at least forty-four thousand years or more.

Drone Nation by Christopher B. Dillworth
Are we all on autopilot? When was the last time you felt like *you* were in control instead of some enlisted geek who goes home to barbecue at the end of the day after guiding you to do his evil bidding?

CHALLAHDAYS

Thanksgivukkah is a holiday name given to the convergence of the American holiday of Thanksgiving and the first day of the Jewish holiday of Hanukkah.

—Wikipedia

Now, this is the fifth time I've celebrated Hanukkah as president. But this is my first Thanikkah—did I say that right?" Obama said during his opening remarks, trying to spit out the word Thanksgivukkah"

—*Boston* magazine

MORE JEWISH/AMERICAN COMBINED HOLIDAYS:

Good Enough Friday

Look Who's Independence Day

Call Your Mother's Day

Chinese Takeout New Year

Kosher Groundhog Day

Valentines Schmalentines

Ash Whatever

Marty Luther King, CPA, Day

My Son the President's Day

Saint Purim's Day

April Meshuganahs' Day

Palmover Sunday

Easter, Big Whoop

Enough Already Easter Monday

Everything's Wront

Such a Flag Day

Maybe, Maybe Not Day

Oy, the Labor Day

What's with the Mask Day?

Columbus Is Nice Day

Coast Guard Veterans Day

Christmitzvah

Kwanzanukkah

Cinco de Matzo

Nana in Corpus Christi Day

Yom-a-Ramadan

Feast of the Immaculate Kitchen

Sy, Bert, Monday

Lincoln Continental's Birthday

Just an Assumption Day

Murray Thursday

Arbor Hashanah Day

Marty Gras, CPA, Day

Pre-need Memorial Day

Pentabelowcost Sunday

Supposedly Your Father's Day

Mr. Big Shot Patriot's Day

Simple Black Friday

Pearl Schwartz Day

D for Discount Day

Thankshavuot Day

What's So Super Bowl Sunday

DISCARDED CHRIS CHRISTIE CAMPAIGN SLOGANS

- Let Me Eat Cake
- The Only Thing We Have to Fear Is No Buffet
- I Like Food
- Frosting You Can Believe In
- Keep Dinner Reservations Alive
- Turning Swords into Forks
- Two Chickens on Every Plate
- Feel the Bulge
- Let's Get America Snacking
- The Longest Journey Starts with a Decent Meal
- Christie Kreme

- Power to the Lunch
- Give Cheese a Chance
- Remember the Crème Brûlée
- The Mallomar Stops Here
- Stay the Three-Course Meal
- Cheesy Fondue and Crab Cakes, Too
- Don't Change Forks in the Middle of a Meal
- Ma, Ma, Where's My Pie?
- Four More Helpings
- We Want Dessert
- Peace and Profiteroles
- It's the Lemon Meringue, Stupid
- Yes We Can Stuff Ourselves
- Breakfast Again in America
- Read My Lips: No More Dieting
- Are You Better Off Than You Were Without Syrup?
- Dinner First
- Eat, Baby, Eat
- In Your Heart, You Know He's Got Cookies
- Keep Cool and Keep Eating
- Putting Dessert First
- We Want Seconds
- Give Me Liberty or Give Me Lunch
- He Ain't Heavy, It's Just My Back Fat
- Win with Snacks
- Keep Cinnabon Alive
- Move Forward at the Buffet
- Christie Delivers Takeout

Everything's Wront

- Power to the Pie
- Nobody Can Swallow Trump
- Don't Change Lanes in the Middle of a Bridge
- Bypass Trump, Vote for Christie
- I Am Not a Whore
- Fewer Indictments Than Hillary
- Chris Christie, for Chrissakes
- Sweatin' for Christie
- Food You Can Believe In
- Make Chris Christie Fat Again

DOGTV

Welcome to DOGTV—the first television channel for dogs. DOGTV is scientifically developed and pup approved. DOGTV is the first television network for dogs that is created exclusively for canines…"The content is not for human eyes," Levi said. "It might be clear to dogs but not necessarily to people."

—DOGTV website

PROGRAM GUIDE

7:00   The Morning Walk: Buster Tries to Pick Up after Himself
7:15   One Life to Leash

Everything's Wront

7:30	All My Chew Toys
8:00	General Veterinary
8:15	Dr. Paws: Who's a Good Boy?
8:30	The Bark
9:00	Get the Ball
9:15	Curb Your Dog. Today: Surviving the Guilt of Lying on the Couch
9:30	Project Runaway. Today: Alone in the City without a License or a Chip
10:00	Worms of the Rich and Famous
10:15	The Art of the Beg
10:30	Rolling Over with Dignity
11:00	The Anticipation Show. Today: Being Cool in the Elevator *Before* the Door Opens
11:15	Sit! What's Up with Your Master?
11:30	The Master Whisperer
12:00	Packs of Los Angeles
12:15	Dog Walkers Unleashed: Do They Play Favorites?
12:45	Down, Boy: Canine Meds and You
1:00	Lapdogs and Lhasa Apsos
1:30	Gender Bending at the Vet: Don't Get "Put Down" While Being Spayed
1:45	Altered States
2:00	The Fixer: Can You Still Lick That Place Where Your Balls Used to Be?
2:15	Mad Dogs
2:30	My Mother Was a Wolf
3:00	Fetching with Dignity

3:15	On Point
3:30	The Retrievers. Today's Topic: Gun Control
3:45	The View
4:00	The Joy of Shedding
4:15	Last Canine Barking
4:30	700 Kennel Club
10:00	Lifestyles of the Rich and Pedigreed
10:30	Run, Chief, Run
11:00	Off the Leash with Cha-Cha
11:30	Paws of Life
12:00	News with Rachel Maddog
12:30	Mixed Breed. Today's Topic: Are Obama's Dogs African American?
1:00	Dog Food: The Ten-Second Meal in a Can
1:30	The Treat: Is Begging Justified?
2:00	The Explainer. Today: The True Meaning of "Gimme Your Paw"
2:30	NOVA. Today: Fish in the Dish: Too Jewish?
3:00	Collars: Dogs Fighting Crime
3:15	The License Game: Contestants Compete for Treats
3:30	Bad Dog: Law and Order in the Doghouse
4:00	Stay! The No-Travel Show
4:30	Dog Run. Today: The Invisible Fence: NSA Abuse or Legitimate Boundary?
5:00	Scraps. Today: Dining Under the Table
6:00	Movie: *Endless Journey: When Your Owner Is Homeless*
6:30	Movie: *Dog Day Afternoon*

7:00	DMTV: "Who Let The Dogs Out?" "It's Raining Postmen"
7:15	The Big Sniff. Today: Performance Anxiety and Fire Hydrants
7:30	Paw Stars
7:45	Rover Chicken
8:00	Chasing Cars: Do You Really Want One?
8:15	SpongeToy SquarePants
8:30	Bones
9:00	Wheel of Bacon
9:30	Doghouse, MD. Today: Dr. Doghouse Bites a Patient
10:00	Garbage Ultimatum
11:00	The Real Bitches of New Jersey
11:30	Bitch, Bitch, Bitch: Talk Show for Females
12:00	Movie: *Howl*
12:30	Dog, the Bounty Hunter
1:00	You Be Good
1:10	Cats!

FIRST LINES OF THE EULOGY FOR ARCH WEST—THE INVENTOR OF DORITOS

- We've come here, not to bury Arch, but to give him one last dip.
- Arch was such a multifaceted guy; I bet we can't bury him just once.
- Arch West was the salt of the earth, and most of it came from his chips.
- He was a man who was proud to be called "cheesy."
- Arch West: A chip off the old cornmeal.

- Arch was proud to be a bagman for Doritos…and sometimes two.
- Arch is dead, but his body's not stiff…it's just crunchier than most.
- Arch is survived by his loving wife, his two daughters, and a large bowl of guacamole.
- Arch has gone to that big onion dip in the sky.
- Arch's invention occupies a special place in the hearts and bypasses of all Americans.
- Arch West…gone but not digested.
- As we say good-bye to Arch, let the chips fall where they may.
- Arch West is dead, but his many fans are comforted in knowing that his remains were toasted, not cremated.
- Arch West. The man came up with the greatest combination of corn and cheese since *Hee Haw*.

DRONE DELIVERY

I recently did some shopping on Amazon and signed up for its new Prime Air. Here's a log of how it went.

7:00 a.m.—Woke up early and remembered that I needed a new brush head for my electric toothbrush. Sure, I could still get by with the old one, but they say change 'em every three months. I think it's been six years. I go on Amazon. Click, click, and *One-Click*. Three new brush heads are on their way. Boy, am I glad I signed up for Prime Air. Thanks, Jeff Bezos.

7:35—While waiting for my brushes, I remember that everybody's talking about that new novel *The Goldfinch*, and I haven't read it yet. So I go back on Amazon and order it on the spot. It feels good to know that Prime Air will have that sucker in my hands before the day is out.

8:13—Nothing yet, and nothing overhead. I look up and see contrails, but I figure it's just an SAC bomber patrolling the North Atlantic corridor, and not my electric-toothbrush brush heads. So I go back on Amazon and click "Where's my stuff?" "Kentucky," it says. "In transit," it says. Oh boy. But while I'm checking, I see something that "others who bought electric toothbrush brush heads bought." Knee Hockey. The kids would love it. I order a set as a surprise because, with Prime Air, I know it will be here today. I wonder if Knee Hockey is anything like the kind of sex I used to have. Still no delivery.

10:07—You know how sometimes you say, "As the crow flies"? That's what Prime Air is like. Forget trucks, roads, conveyor belts, and forklifts. I got a drone coming, baby, and it's bringing me my stuff posthaste. I go outside, and this thing with four propellers is circling my house. About one thousand feet up. It's lost and can't find the house. I can't yell because it's a drone. I can't wave because how would it know it's me? So I just stand there while this bug thing circles. Forever. Finally, I go back inside.

10:54—The drone-delivery vehicle has been up there for almost an hour. Around and around it circles, as if it's got nothing else better to do. It isn't even getting lower. Now I realize I'm going to have to put my address on my roof to get my drone deliveries. But then I think, *How will it know?* And if I do that, the police helicopters will probably raid me. It'll be worse than Patty Hearst. Prime Air is great, but there may be glitches.

11:38—I get in the car to take my shoes to the shoemaker. I can't wait all day. I have a life. I also ordered napkins on Amazon. It's pretty addictive. Then I saw something Amazon suggested I buy with the napkins. A Cuisinart blender. They are "often ordered together." So I took Amazon up on it, along with the Prime Air delivery and all. But I still have to get my shoes to the shoemaker. So I drive down my driveway and turn onto the street. I'm heading toward the strip mall where the cobbler is, when all of a sudden, "Bam!" I hear this thing land on the roof of my car. I pull over and get out. There are my electric-toothbrush brush heads delivered right on top of my car. And I see this thing with four propellers hovering over the package like it was laying eggs or something. Or like it was protecting its young. What am I supposed to say? Thank you? It's a *machine*, for crissakes. A drone. It doesn't take tips. Next thing I know, before I can do anything, it flies off. Just like that. Zip, and it's gone. No signature. My box of electric toothbrush brush heads is on top of my car. The thing couldn't have landed in my driveway like a normal delivery—or maybe, even, while I was home? Or left it leaning up against the garage in the rain for a week? Thanks, Jeff.

12:10—Then I make a mistake. I go on Amazon and order a Sunday Missal. I'm Catholic. What the hell? I lost my old Missal when I was playing Father Damien in a leprosy pageant for the CYO. I need the new Missal in time for Sunday Mass, so I opt for Prime Air again. Big mistake.

3:46—I am napping on the couch when it hits. A Hellfire missile pierces my roof and explodes in the attic. Makes a helluva racket. Apparently, Jeff Bezos means business. The attic is destroyed, but the missile misses me. Strangely, I'm not mad or anything, just surprised. What the hell is going on? Fortunately, I'm able to gather enough of the Hellfire parts to ask for a return. "Not what I ordered," I click.

4:50—I print out the return label and authorization number. I find a box, pack everything in it, and seal it. I feel like maybe I should return the thing by air, but I think better of it and take it down to UPS instead. The UPS guy wants to know if it's a return. I feel like saying, "How about a retaliation, if you get my drift." But I think better of that, too. "Just a return," I say. "No charge," he says. "All paid for." Thank you, Jeff Bezos.

5:42—Bezos completely misunderstands my return. He must think I'm getting hostile, like an insurgent. He thinks I want a replacement Missal. I do. So, this time he sends me back two Hellfires, and the drone releases them on my house from about fifteen hundred feet. Suddenly, Prime Air doesn't like to come down to earth when it delivers. Luckily I wasn't home or I would've been killed. I guess the Prime Air drone doesn't always know everything about some of its recipients. My place is completely destroyed. Thanks for the speedy return, Jeff Bezos. And where's my copy of *The Goldfinch*, my napkins, the Cuisinart blender, and my Knee Hockey?

6:02—I get an e-mail. It says the Prime Air drone from Amazon can no longer find my house because of the Missal/missile mix-up. Prime Air doesn't deliver to rubble.

6:17—Prime Air can't find my house. *I* can't find my house. But when I go outside, I see the drone thing circling at about five thousand feet. Just circling, not delivering. If it can't find the house, then what is it looking for? Or looking at? I think Prime Air's got something else in mind.

7:28—I try to "pick up the pieces," as they say, and go on with my life, Prime Air or no Prime Air. I know the drone is up there, but what the hell? So are a lot of other things that can hurt you. Like God, for starters. I don't even want to think about that.

Next Day
2:45 p.m.—"Where's My Stuff?" I click again on Amazon. My house is destroyed. The neighbors think I'm a terrorist

and are afraid to come over. They figure Prime Air might deliver a couple of Hellfires just to be collateral about it. Nobody comes to the cat's funeral because funerals are just the kind of thing Prime Air likes to deliver to. I'm all alone.

Three Days Later
10:20 a.m.—Amazon still hasn't answered my "Where's My Stuff?" click. The Prime Air drone is still overhead, but it's so high now I can't tell if it's carrying anything. How could it stay aloft for so long holding a Cuisinart blender? Is there no decency? And what about my Knee Hockey, napkins, and the hardcover copy of *The Goldfinch*?

One Week Later
4:12 p.m.—I'm sitting in a lawn chair outside the remains of my house when very quietly—I mean, *very* quietly—the Prime Air drone thing lands about fifty feet from where I'm sitting. Sort of at the edge of the driveway, down where it blends into the street. You wouldn't have heard it if you hadn't seen it. It comes straight down like a dragonfly and rests there as if it has no weight on its legs. So even standing, it still looks like it's hovering. All drones are like that. Even the ones with wings. But I swear—*my hand to God*—I swear it's trying to tell me it's sorry. The drone. A fucking *machine*. It's sorry about the Missal/missile mix-up and the Hellfires and all the death and destruction in the name of same-day delivery. It's even sorry about the 24-7 surveillance afterward.

I'm not reading into this. This is what it's like. We look at each other for a long time, me and the Prime Air drone. Just thinking, I guess. I know that's what *I*'m doing. Who the hell knows what a drone does when it's not delivering? Maybe just computing, I guess. Measuring me and everything around me and figuring out the algorithms of it all. Neither one of us wants to make the first move.

4:56—Finally, I get up, fold the lawn chair, and walk into the garage—the one that used to be attached to my house. When I get in out of the sun, I turn around and look back at the drone. Just a glance, that's all. The thing's engines start up again with a soft whir. And then v-e-r-y slowly, it lifts off the driveway apron and sort of tilts toward me in my direction. Nothing hostile, mind you. But real human-like. I stand there and wait for it to come close. It hesitates at first, and then it flies into the garage with me. I press the automatic garage-door-opener button and bring the garage door down. Then I turn on the lights. And now it's just me and the drone, alone and private. I think it's actually tired of all the Prime Air bullshit. It just wants to come down to earth and be done with it. I feel like, maybe, I should hug it—but then, the propellers and all. It understands.

Next Day
8:55 a.m.—I click "Where's My Stuff?" and tell Amazon to forget it. I cancel the Knee Hockey, Cuisinart blender,

napkins, and *The Goldfinch*. Who needs that stuff? Especially *The Goldfinch*. Nobody I know who has read it, liked it, so why spend the money?

Three Weeks Later
9:15 p.m.—We don't go out much, the drone and me. But at the same time, it's still not much help around the garage, either. It can't do anything except be what it is: a drone. In the end, though, it's OK as company, and it's definitely no trouble. But right now, I'm trying to figure out why I'm living with it in my garage. It seems happy just being there and doing nothing—like a drone, or Al Gore. But where does it all end? I guess, for the drone at least, now it's mainly just "prime time" instead of Prime Air. Thanks, Jeff Bezos.

GLITCHES IN MY PROGRAM, OR SOMETHING'S WRONT

"Sir, it *felt* like you were breaking the speed limit. You know, sorta like a wind-chill temperature." [System Fail]

"When you say 'retainer,' is that a thing for your teeth or just up-front money?" [Page Not Found]

"Brain surgery isn't my specialty." [No Network Connection]

"Mother broke her hip. She's not going to sue, but she needs to stay longer." [Not Responding]

"Tommy and me play 'gay doctor' all the time." [Restart Now]

"Dad! Mom said I'd never find you. Is your new name French?" [Mailer Daemon]

"There may be a *little* botulism in *some* of the chicken salad." [Restore Settings to an Earlier Time]

"We've decided to go in a different direction." [Driver Not Found]

"I don't like the looks of that." [File Corrupted]

"Hold this while I check the connection." [Fatal Error]

"Is it hot in here, or is it just my tinfoil?" [Request Timed Out]

"That was cat food. The marlin pâté is in the fridge." [Download Failure]

"I'm sorry. I thought *you* were the one who was waiting for chemo. [No Response]

"Hitler went too far." [Network Authentication Required]

"How about Twister?" [Not Responding]

"We're lookin' at just a little itty-bitty bit o' turbulence up ahead, so we're gonna ask y'all, at this time, to just kinda fasten your seat belts right about now if y'all don't mind. Flight attendants cross-check and prepare for water landing." [Reboot Now]

"It's not a hostage situation till they want something." [No Network Access]

"You wanna go through the park?" [Access Denied]

"Don't worry. He's very friendly." [System Fail]

"Dad, I bought the new sports car with all my babysitting money." [No Connection]

"I'm not following you. This is the way I go home." [Limited Access]

"It's not assisted living. It's rehab." [Service Unavailable]

"We're being held momentarily." [Abort, Retry, Fail?]

"May cause vomiting, headaches, nausea, excessive bleeding, loss of appetite, suicidal thoughts, reduced motor control, dry skin, hair loss, swelling, hearing impairment, and death." [Bad Command or File Name]

"Swipe again. No additional charges will incur." [File Corrupted]

"Before we take off, we're going to dump some fuel just in case." [Invalid Username or Password]

"Objects in mirror are closer than they appear." [Reset]

"A donation has been made in your name." [Request Timed Out]

"This call may be recorded." [Out of Memory]

"…Nigeria." [System Restore]

"Park thoughtfully." [Upgrade Required]

"Breathe normally." [Retry]

"If this is an emergency, hang up." [Not Logged In]

"The last four digits of your Social Security number." [Wait Ten Seconds, Then Restart]

"This happens all the time." [Request Header Too Large]

"You'll be fine." [No Connection]

"Would you like earplugs for this procedure?" [Unauthorized]

"Do you mean *I'm* breaking up, or *we're* breaking up?" [Missing File]

"You may feel a slight discomfort." [User Identification Failed]

"We have to talk." [Troubleshoot Problems]

HOROSCOPE

ARIES

Get ready for love this month. With Venus traversing your Pluto, even a "closing time" dog could prick your fancy. But be careful. Even though you might appreciate a great butt, you don't want to butt heads with the bartender who's invested a night's worth of free drinks in that woolly mammoth and expects to reap the benefits. Just remember: sometimes a ram is just a lamb with a hard head. If you plan to travel this month, walk. Jupiter is opposing Venus, so when your mate desires some TLC, don't show up in bed with a finger puppet. Just remember: the best comb-over in the world starts in a bad place.

TAURUS

Sometimes you're headstrong like a bull, and sometimes you're just full of it. Mars moves into your Seventh House, the one with the pool. Right now, confusion reigns. So rather than go charging off in every direction, it might be best to sit back and let somebody else do the "chopsticks in your mouth like a walrus" bit. You've been feeling neglected lately, but have patience. Mercury goes from retrograde to upgrade on the tenth, and you'll be filled with new energy and may even be able to finally watch all of *Inside Llewyn Davis* without saying, "WTF?" Won't *that* be fun! Stay away from porcupines. You could die from a thousand little pricks—sort of like dating Menudo. Avoid playing catch with anyone who's projectile vomiting.

GEMINI

It's not easy being "twins." When Noah had his ark, you would've shown up as "one." Inside, you're a total mess even though outside everyone thinks you resemble Justin Bieber with a goiter condition. This month brings new hope in the form of a full moon and Jupiter transiting your Seventh House. With the moon in Mercury, those twins you thought you were sleeping with turn out to be just a bad pair of glasses. Now is the time to grab the kids and sell them to the nearest gypsy, if you can. Live a little. You deserve it. After all, you did your time in hell, you need a little R&R—Ritalin and Resuscitation. The twenty-fourth brings the arrival of an extraterrestrial creature. Then your wife agrees to a conjugal visit.

CANCER
Cancers are never satisfied, no matter how many batteries they steal from their kids' toys. This month is no exception. Venus rules. And you will find that love is just around the corner, even if it's only just some *E. coli* from getting into a hot tub with Mickey Rourke. Money seems to gravitate toward you, no matter what. Now is the time to invest. Throw caution to the wind and refinance your mortgage with a loan shark named Nunzio. You've earned it. The end of the month will reveal the answer to the question that has been nagging you all year long: *When Miley Cyrus does that thing with her tongue, does it ever attract flies?* The moon is entering Pisces. Time to turn over a new leaf. Try not wearing swaddling clothes to the office for a change.

LEO
Something wonderful is in store for you this month. You have been overworked at the office and overlooked at home. Maybe you *shouldn't* wear overalls to bed. And mudpacks are usually worn on the *face*. But now, with lugubrious Saturn finally leaving your birth sign, you could shoot your mouth off at a school for the deaf if you felt like it. When Mercury squares your moon, you will discover that having sex with a Venus flytrap is a felony in most states. But go ahead. Just be careful not to overindulge,

or you'll learn that while love is never having to say you're sorry, marriage, on the other hand, is like having Apology Tourette's. Stop chanting "I'm doing number one" every time you relieve yourself in public. Mercury in retrograde causes you to think that a woman giving birth looks like Ho Chi Minh eating a football.

VIRGO

Good news, all you Virgos. The buzz you've been feeling lately turns out to be just the antitheft device you left clamped to the underwear you stole from Big and Tall last month. Remember: you have nothing to fear but fear itself, and, of course, that guy next door who owns a Jaw Saw. With Venus conjoining with Uranus, now is the time to take your dust-ball collection to *Antiques Roadshow* and claim you had "no idea." Neptune finally enters your Sixth House just in time to bring some much-needed relief for that nasty tongue rash that appeared during the lunar eclipse through no fault of your own. Take heart. This month sees a brand-new you, if someone would only buy you a drink.

LIBRA

Everyone thinks Libras are so even-keeled, but "the scales" this month refer to that nasty outbreak of psoriasis on your back. But don't worry. The scales will tip both ways for you this month, thanks to Neptune squaring your Venus, and Jupiter acting like a complete douchebag. This is a good time to put off any major purchases such as a new house or Canadian Viagra. When the new moon makes its appearance on the twelfth, it might be a good time to finally mention your personal trainer's nasty habit of farting while counting backward. Your feet may swell as a result of Pluto in retrograde. On the other hand, it could also be due to those nutcrackers you left in your ballet slippers. Either way, avoid any ugly confrontations such as homicidal maniacs, pestilences, or being trapped in a rowboat with Alan Greenspan. Saturn takes a header on the fifteenth, and your career as the mascot of a semipro women's softball team suddenly seems like a real possibility. Time to clean those questionable stains off your chicken suit.

SCORPIO

Mars and Venus are battling it out over their summer rental in your Third House. It's always about sex with you. This month brings a double whammy of unbridled sexual attraction, and binge viewing of all eight seasons of *Who's the Boss?*—something only a Scorpio, accustomed to self-inflicted wounds, could do. When Pluto arrives at midheaven, Virgo provides nasty thoughts of finally telling that "no parking" lady at LAX where to go. Scorpios are famous for loving and leaving—often without paying. But be careful not to overdo it when it comes to hair replacement or affairs of the heart. The stars impel, they don't compel—except, maybe, Barbra Streisand. The conjunction of Mars and Mercury in your Fifth House could cause trouble, especially if you haven't changed the sheets. Warning: your penis is not a ventriloquist's dummy. Resist drawing eyes on it with a Sharpie. And just remember, when everything seems completely hopeless, you're right.

SAGITTARIUS
You call yourself "the archer," but your quiver looks like Robin Quivers. Pluto, your ruling planet, indicates that the money you spent at the gym last month would have been better spent on a hooker with a sharp stick. Everyone thinks you're happy-go-lucky, but you're the guy who looks down at himself in the men's room at a ball game and asks, "Is that all there is?" Don't worry. Your day will come. Travel is likely this month. Possibly to the Far East, where vaginas are small and language is no barrier. Your customary sunny disposition will be tested when Saturn plops itself down defiantly in your Fifth House. Try Mexican food. You could use a little spice in your life, even if it is just a jalapeño high colonic. And remember, you can run but you can't hide, especially from AARP.

CAPRICORN
Venus rules, so give yourself a break and remember: STP is a fuel additive; *STD* is a sexually transmitted disease. That is, unless you really, really like your Buick. It's time to come out from under the covers, wake up, and smell the faint aroma of burned rubber coming from your partner's orthopedic strap-on. Mercury goes direct, which

means that when people tell you you're too short or your back looks like Michael Jackson's former chimp, you can believe them. But beware. That AK-47 you've been keeping under your pillow could prove embarrassing when you try to convince Homeland Security you thought Al was the first name of a cute guy named "Qaeda" you met on eHarmony. The planets know best. Your Venus aligning with Mars will make you wish you hadn't lost your virginity in a mosh pit.

AQUARIUS
Your magnanimous personality will change this month from thoughts of world peace to finally deciding to take a Zumba class to learn how to twerk. Your ruling planet, Uranus, is just about ready to give up the ghost and call it a prostate exam as it moves into your Ninth House. This can only mean one thing: no more French dip for lunch. Aquarians love everyone yet never seem to catch anything. Even so, it behooves you to button up your overcoat—especially when you shoplift. Someone you love reveals himself as a serial killer this month, but you take it all in stride and chalk it up as just his inability to commit. The full moon brings a great business opportunity in the form of second-story work in a wealthy neighborhood. The moon traversing your Eighth House will make it harder for you to break up with a loved one without first introducing her to a tailor who thinks *Lord of the Flies* is about pants.

PISCES

Pisces is one of the most misunderstood signs of the Zodiac. Pisces have a reputation for being heavy drinkers. Yet the fact is, they make the *other* signs heavy drinkers. With the sun entering your Ninth House, there's no telling what it will be this month: feast or famine, or a little of both—like pigging out on Weight Watchers. There is a strong possibility that an old love will reappear toward the end of the month but hopefully she won't be lactating, or armed with a restraining order. Money comes your way in the form of the winning purse in a shepherd's-pie cooking contest using real dogs.

HORSE DRAWN OUT

Thank you all for coming out on such a cold morning. These are the days when I'm glad I have a blanket. I will make this brief. This is not about the mayor's plan to get rid of all the horse-drawn carriages at the Plaza, even though I think we'd be better served if he got rid of all the prostitutes first. But, apparently, he thinks those are just whores of a different color. Sorry. A little cold-morning humor there.

Anyway, the reason I've called you here today is for an announcement I would like to make. The time seems right for me. I know the time is right for the city and right for the horse-drawn-carriage business as a whole. And regardless of how it may affect my status as one of the top draft horses this year, I have something to say.

OK. Here goes.

I am a gay horse. I've been a gay horse ever since I was a colt, and long before I ever started working in Central Park with horse-drawn carriages. My stablemates have always known I was gay, and I have never hidden it from them, but now you in the press, the city, and maybe even the world will know that I am gay. And I'm OK with that. Because now I'm free. Except, maybe, for the fact that I have to stand around here all day like an idiot with a bag of oats around my neck and this dumb carriage attached to my ass.

Anyway, I hope now we can all get on with our lives. I plan to get on with the rest of my life as a top draft horse here in New York, the greatest city in the world. I know in my heart I have more to contribute than just being a horse that is gay. My homosexuality does not define me even though that is what I am. I don't really want to be the Jackie Robinson of horses. I just want to be who I am and lead a normal life. Although this fucking carriage and the standing and waiting and all those dumb tourists drive me nuts. So, please, from now on, I'm just a horse. OK? Who happens to be gay. If I am the first openly gay horse in the carriage business, so be it. I don't know about Aqueduct or Belmont. That's none of my business. I'm sure there are gay thoroughbreds out there. Why not? But if they want to live a lie and pretend to be studs, I can only say to them that coming out has been liberating for me and has made me the happiest horse in New York.

Enough said. Thank you very much.

REPORTER: Do you think being gay will affect your future as a draft-horse prospect in New York?
HORSE: That's not for me to say. My ability is the same today as it was yesterday before I came out. If it bothers some people, that's their problem. People don't have to be afraid to ride with me. I've heard all the jokes about "side-saddle" and "double gaited." They're actually very funny. Even I whinny sometimes when I hear them. But I'm just like any other horse.
REPORTER: Are you worried about how other horses in the stable will treat you now?
HORSE: Not really. I've never had a problem with that in any stable I've ever been in.
REPORTER: Are you attracted to other horses?
HORSE: Sure. Aren't you? But I don't mix business with mounting.
REPORTER: What did your stablemates say when you told them you were gay?
HORSE: I didn't tell them. They all knew. I never hid my sexuality from anybody. But I guess the fact that they never saw me with a filly or in any of their stud magazines probably tipped them off. It was never a big deal.
REPORTER: Can you still be a stud?
HORSE: Sure. Aren't we all?
REPORTER: You know what I mean. What about when they put you out to pasture? Will you still work as a stud?
HORSE: Well, probably not. You know what they say: "You can lead a horse to water…" But, honestly, I don't think it's

anyone's business. What happens when I go back to the stable or out in a pasture is my private business.

REPORTER: What about on the job, pulling carriages? Do you think people will refuse to ride in your carriage because you're gay?

HORSE: It's never come up. Most tourists just want to enjoy the ride. People don't want to know whether the horse that's pulling their carriage is gay or straight. My sexuality doesn't affect my job as a draft horse. If you suddenly found out your car was gay, would that change the way you treated it or drove it to work?

REPORTER: I don't know. Maybe when I filled it up with gas. I mean, where would I stick the nozzle?

HORSE: How about in the gas tank where you usually put it?

REPORTER: But I'm not gay.

HORSE: Congratulations. I feel sorry for you.

REPORTER: Why?

HORSE: Because when you get married, it'll probably be to a woman.

REPORTER: Do you have something against traditional marriage?

HORSE: Not at all. I'm all for it. But I think we gays get the better end of the deal. No pun intended. Henny Youngman never said, "Take my husband…" But I don't want to get into a discussion about gay marriage. To me it's a nonissue. And I think the courts are finally coming

around to that. I just wanted to clear the air about me as a horse.
REPORTER: That's another thing. Why do horses have to shit in the street? Is that a gay thing?
HORSE: Next question.
REPORTER: What does your driver think?
HORSE: He's for anything that makes me happy and keeps me working. Although I have noticed he's a little easier with the whip ever since he found out I was homosexual. But I don't necessarily think that's right, either. The whip is as much a part of being a horse as having a bit in your mouth. It has nothing to do with being gay. It has to do with being a horse.
REPORTER: Maybe he's gay.
HORSE: I wouldn't know.
REPORTER: If your driver were gay, would that be OK with you?
HORSE: What do you want me to say? "It'd be fabulous?" Look. The man spends all day staring at my ass. Does that make him gay? Again, you'd have to ask him. I don't know what he likes. I haven't got eyes in the back of my head.
REPORTER: How many other carriage horses are gay?
HORSE: I'm sure there are others. Actually, I know there are. But that's for them to say, not me. I only speak for myself. All I know is I'm a gay horse. It doesn't affect the way I pull a carriage, and shouldn't affect my worth as a draft horse in general.

REPORTER: Just to be clear on all this. You really don't think your announcement today will change the way the other horses treat you?
HORSE: I don't think it's a big surprise to anyone who knows me. If they were going to treat me differently, that would have happened a long time ago. Actually, the only ones I have to worry about are people like you.
REPORTER: If you're a gelding, does that make you gay?
HORSE: That's actually a good question. The truth is, I'm a gelding. Which, by the way, takes care of that earlier "stud" question. But having your balls cut off doesn't affect who you are. Only what you do. I'm a gay gelding. But gelding isn't gay, and gay is not gelding. I guess I should be happy I can still pull a carriage.
REPORTER: What about the other New York horses? Have you been in touch with them?
HORSE: You mean, like thoroughbreds? Or police horses? Or the show horses in Westchester County? There are probably as many gay horses among them as there are gay jockeys, police officers, or show riders. But for the life of me, I couldn't tell you which ones are which.
REPORTER: Would you call Mitt Romney's horse gay?
HORSE: Look. Prancing does not make you gay. That's like saying all prancers and trotters are gay. That's just dumb. Being gay is like having chestnut hair. It's something you're born with. There are plenty of heterosexual prancers out there. Just ask the mares. Where do you think all the prancing colts come from? All I know is that

Everything's Wront

I'm going to be happier and a much better draft horse because of what I've done today.

    Thank you, gentlemen.
REPORTER: One more question.
HORSE: OK, shoot.
REPORTER: How do you spell "*draught*"?

LGBTWHA?

LGBT may also include additional Qs for "queer" or "questioning" (sometimes abbreviated with a question mark, and sometimes used to mean anybody not literally L, G, B, or T), which can then look like, e.g., LGBTQ or LGBTQQ. Other variants may add a U for "unsure"; a C for "curious"; an I for "intersex"; another T for "transsexual" or "transvestite"; another T, TS, or 2 for "two-spirit" persons; an A or SA for "straight allies"; or an A for "asexual." Some may also add a P for "pansexual" or "polyamorous," an H for "HIV-affected," and/or an O for "other."

—Wikipedia

Z. People who sleep through sex.
W. People who have sex with "wrong numbers" instead of simply hanging up.

N.	Nongenital sex partners.
C.	Those who have sex only with people who misspell words on Craigslist.
K.	Any Kardashian.
TX.	Orgasmic sexters.
BO.	People who forgo deodorant as a contraceptive.
LN.	People who insist on sex during late-night monologues.
P.	Women who own more than two cats.
PP.	Men who think they can have sex with women who own more than two cats.
AP.	People who choose to have sex with frozen food.
LT.	Heterosexuals in long-term marriages.
GA.	People who use kitchen utensils as sexual aids.
GE.	People who use electrical appliances as sexual objects.
CB.	Role-players from regional theater.
F.	Those who thirst for bodily fluids.
V.	People who prefer sex with balls (not testicles).
K.	Social directors who have "Simon Says" sex.
D.	Masturbators who cheat on themselves.
O.	Oral Roberts University dropouts.
PJ.	Newscasters who say, "This just in."
X.	People attracted to ex-partners with restraining orders.
SS.	People whose orgasms consist of saying, "Are you finished yet?" or "What time does the L train stop running?"
R.	Sexual staplers who only use Swingline.

LL. Sexual looky-loos who waste everybody's time.
H. Men who have been told they're too short even though they're of normal height.
AT. People who have "phone sex" with actual phones.
J. Individuals with sexually deviated septums.
GOP. Republicans.
SCP. People who are sexually attracted to cereal-box characters.
HM. People who hum during orgasms.
RP. Rappers with speech impediments.
TY. Nude transvestites.
XB. Vegetarians who eschew oral sex for ethical reasons.
SLX. Stoplight exhibitionists.
S. People who prefer sex standing up (elevators and subways).
ALZ. Alzheimer's patients who can't remember where anything goes.
SL. People for whom sex is shopping with a credit card other than their own.
NS. Nymphomaniac shut-ins.
NK. Unassimilated North Koreans with bad haircuts.
BY. Buy-sexuals.
CD. Designer-only cross-dressers.
WW. Window washers who can't commit.
ST. Siamese twins with separation anxiety.
PWP. Wet-parts body piercers.
VX. Nearsighted voyeurs.
QT. People with pet names for sexual organs.

Everything's Wront

C. Tabletop artists.
DS. Individuals who like sex with nontraditional parts of their bodies.
KY. People who believe K-Y Jelly has something to do with Kentucky.
AL. Al Roker.
GX. People who remove their glasses to weigh themselves but don't remove them for sex.

MADOFF MADNESS

"I don't know whose idea it was, but we decided to kill ourselves… We took pills and woke up the next day…I'm glad I woke up…I'm not sure how I feel about him waking up."
—Ruth Madoff, in the *New York Times*

> AT RISE: A luxury bedroom in New York City. Mid-December 2008. BERNIE MADOFF and his wife, RUTH, have just returned home.

RUTH
I can't believe this is happening. This is horrendous.

BERNIE
A hundred and fifty years. That's two life sentences.

RUTH
Thank God you can serve them simultaneously.

BERNIE
It's over.

RUTH
The whole thing, Bernie. The money's just part of it. But the phone calls, the e-mails, the angry emoticons. I'm at the end of my rope. I have had enough, Bernie Madoff. I don't know why you're so calm.

BERNIE
I have to go back to the office.

RUTH
For what? To steal some more? I am a wreck.

BERNIE
To finish up things.

RUTH
We've already been to the office. For the Christmas party. Half an hour. That was plenty. And what's to celebrate? We're Jewish, and you stole 65 billion dollars. This whole scandal has just added to my depression, if you know what I mean.

BERNIE
I know what you mean.

RUTH
Bernie, don't go back to the office. I don't want you leaving this place. I want you to stay right here with me.

BERNIE
Then let's go to bed.
(He lies down heavily on the bed.)

RUTH
Don't tell me you've got something on your mind besides the 65 billion.

BERNIE
Like what?

RUTH
You know.

BERNIE
I'm tired.

RUTH
And just now, when you fell back on the bed like a lunk, the chintz canopy shook like a leaf. I could see huge amounts of dust coming off. You probably didn't notice. But believe me, it was there. A very substantial amount.

BERNIE
So?

RUTH
I'm going to have to fire Esmerelda tomorrow. Christmas or no Christmas. She's not Jewish, so I don't have to worry about Hanukkah.

BERNIE
Don't do that.

RUTH
And the way you're lying there, you look like a corpse with your hands folded. Like you were in a casket or something.

BERNIE
I gotta rest before I go to sleep.

RUTH
I feel half-dead myself from the worrying. Not only that, my feet are killing me. A little rest could do us both some good. And thank God I'm wearing my new gorgeous velour dressing gown you gave me, so lying down is no problem.

BERNIE
Good.
(Ruth lies down, and they are quiet for several long beats.)

RUTH
Bernie?

BERNIE
Yeah?

RUTH
I'm thinking.

BERNIE
What?

RUTH
You ever wish you were dead?

BERNIE
Starting when?

RUTH
Like, starting now.

BERNIE
Sure. Why not?

RUTH
I'm telling you, I really wish I was dead. But I don't want to leave you.

BERNIE
Then go to sleep.

RUTH
That's just it. I can't. Dead would be easier right now, if you know what I mean.

BERNIE
Then take something.

RUTH
No, together. Are you listening to me? "Dead" as in "no more." And we should do it together, or I'm not going through with it.

BERNIE
Through with what?

RUTH
Ending it all. Sayonara. We're outta here.

BERNIE
I don't know. *You* go.

RUTH
Bernie, I have never seen you so unmotivated.

BERNIE
About what?

RUTH
About you and me doing this together. I really think we should take something and just be done with it.

BERNIE
Whatever. Whaddya got?

RUTH
I haven't a clue. Ambien, maybe. Do we have any Ambien?

BERNIE
In my pillbox on the dresser.
(Ruth finds the pillbox.)

RUTH
Since when with the pillbox? You never would buy something like that for yourself. Who gave you the pillbox, Bernie?

BERNIE
You did.

RUTH
I don't recall any pillbox. And Tiffany's, with initials. Hand-engraved, no less. This is a very gorgeous box, Bernie. I swear I never gave this to you. But there's a bunch of pills in here. How am I supposed to know what's what?

BERNIE
What difference does it make?

RUTH
You pick. And, incidentally, it's a lovely box.

BERNIE
They're mostly Ambien, the little white ones.

RUTH
What're the others?

BERNIE
I don't know. Aspirin maybe. Some Lipitor. Nothing important. Mostly Ambien. The white oblong ones with "AMB" on them.

RUTH
How many should we take?

BERNIE
As many as you like.

RUTH
How many are you going to take, Bernie? I'm not investing here. This is supposed to be a mutual effort.

BERNIE
Here. Lemme show you.
(He takes several without looking.)

BERNIE
There. OK? I took some.

RUTH
How many is that? Three? Should I take three? We're talkin' suicide, Bernie. I want to do it right.

BERNIE
Take more than you normally do. Take five times as much.

RUTH
But you only took three. You're bigger than I am.

BERNIE
I'll take more.

RUTH
No, that's OK. Don't splurge on my account. Save some for later.
(She carefully takes two pills.)

RUTH
OK, I'm taking two for starters. There's plenty where that came from.

BERNIE
You won't die with two.

RUTH
But you only took three, and for all I know, you could spit them out. Only do it in a Kleenex so Esmeralda doesn't find them in the morning.

BERNIE
I'm not spitting mine out. You take yours.

RUTH
No, I'm just resting right now. I want to see what it feels like. I can always take more. Like, maybe, you should.

BERNIE
I'll take the whole fucking box if you want.

RUTH
You're not pulling any of that Ponzi nonsense on me, are you, Bernie? I hope I can trust you here. We're doing this as a couple. You better do what you say you're doing.

BERNIE
I took three. I'll take more when you take yours.

RUTH
I took two. And I'll take two more later.

BERNIE
Good. Then it's a deal.

RUTH
Bernie, who gave you the pillbox?

BERNIE
I told you. You did. For my acid reflux.

RUTH
But there's no Nexium in there. You said so yourself.

BERNIE
I don't take that anymore. Aspirin and Ambien and Lipitor. I think the little oval-shaped ones are Lipitor.

RUTH
You don't know for sure? You can't medicate yourself like that, Bernie. It's dangerous.

BERNIE
I know what I'm doing. Trust me. How do you feel?

RUTH
Better.

BERNIE
Take some more.

RUTH
No, I'm OK. Maybe later.

BERNIE
That's not the point.

RUTH
No, two's plenty. You should take another one. Unless you're not serious.

BERNIE
I know what I'm doing. I took three, and I'll give you four when I take another three. And then that's it.

RUTH
Then we'll both have taken six. Is that what you're telling me? Is that what you want?

BERNIE
I'm doing this for you.

RUTH
How do I know it's not one of your schemes? You're pathological, you know.

BERNIE
I know what I'm doing.

RUTH
Well, we'll just see. We can always make our minds up later.
(Bernie rises up and empties the whole box into his mouth.)

BERNIE
OK. There. Now I've put the whole goddamn box in my mouth. You satisfied?

RUTH
That's just great. Now you've taken Ambien, aspirin, and enough Lipitor to reduce your cholesterol to zero. You spit that out right now, Bernie Madoff.
(He spits it out.)

BERNIE
Make up your mind.

RUTH
They're all ruined. So you might as well take what you want because they won't be any good later.

BERNIE
Whatever you say.

RUTH
I'm taking one of the ones you spit out. Thank God we've known each other since I was thirteen. OK, now you.

BERNIE
Ruth…
(He takes several pills.)

RUTH
Good. So what'd you take? Three of the not-Lipitor-looking ones? How do I know they weren't aspirin?

BERNIE
I took whatever I grabbed.

RUTH
We'll have to get another prescription. I can't tell if you're scamming me, but I'm too tired to do anything about it.

BERNIE
I did what you told me.

RUTH
Bernie, let me go to sleep first so I don't have to listen to your snoring.

BERNIE
I can't promise you…

RUTH
And what's the big deal about another prescription? Dr. Katz would fill it in a second. Unless he was an investor.

BERNIE
Yeah, why not?

RUTH
I don't feel a thing.

BERNIE
That's the point.

RUTH
All in all…

BERNIE
What difference does it make if I snore?

RUTH
I'll never get to sleep.

BERNIE
You're trying to kill yourself.

RUTH
Bernie, just let me die in peace. That's all I ask.

BERNIE
OK, but you're gonna have to do it with snoring.

RUTH
If you do…

BERNIE
What?

RUTH
I've been through enough. I don't even know if the pills are full-potency now.

BERNIE
Then take some more.

RUTH
You take some more.

BERNIE
I did. But you made me spit them out. I took them twice.

RUTH
You can never be too sure.

BERNIE
I'm gonna miss this place

RUTH
You know…I've been thinking.

BERNIE
What?

RUTH
Maybe the canopy is a little much. Maybe we should get rid of it and have a normal bed, like people.

BERNIE
It won't change a thing.

RUTH
It never gets cleaned properly, anyway.

BERNIE
Go to sleep.

RUTH
How many pills did you take?

BERNIE
Enough.

RUTH
You scared?

BERNIE
Numb.

RUTH
That's the Ambien.

BERNIE
Don't care.

RUTH
Thank God I didn't take off my makeup.

BERNIE
Makeup?

RUTH
Why? You think I need lipstick?

BERNIE
You're fine.

RUTH
You place your bets, you take your chances.

BERNIE
Win or lose.

RUTH
Win…or lose.

BERNIE
Which?

RUTH
Mostly "win." Look at this place. What's not to like?

BERNIE
Too tired.

RUTH
It's gorgeous.

BERNIE
Sleep.

RUTH
You were always a step ahead.

BERNIE
Lose.

RUTH
Bernie…

BERNIE
More.

RUTH
Bernie…

BERNIE
People.

RUTH
Do you think we should turn out the lights?

Everything's Wront

BERNIE
Don't touch a thing.

RUTH
I can't.

BERNIE
Good.

RUTH
Oh boy.

BERNIE
Am I snoring?

RUTH
Not yet.

BERNIE
A hundred and fifty years.

RUTH
How'd they come up with that?

BERNIE
They added.

RUTH
A hundred and fifty years? No good behavior?

BERNIE
None.

RUTH
Some deal.

BERNIE
A deal's a deal.

RUTH
Well, if you don't wake up, you're a free man.

BERNIE
And if we do?

RUTH
You'll think of something.

BERNIE

Nothing.

(Long pause.)

Maybe the pillbox.

BLACKOUT

MASTERPIECES OF SELF-PUBLISHING

Our Latest Selection

Whips of All Nations (215 pages)
Larry Cox, MD
A leisurely stroll through the history of whips, switches, whisks, whacks, and tails—from buggy to bull, from decorative to decadent. The author delves into his personal collection to provide illustrations, photos, and half-baked justifications. Includes diagrams showing range of motion, and some phone numbers.

How to Skin a Cat (340 pages)
Thomas J. O'Flaherty
From simple Mongolian field dressings to the American way of taxidermy, it's all about getting the job done, no matter what the lame excuse or end result. Many, many ways to skin a feline are discussed in this firsthand account, including the tried and true drilling of a hole in the tail, and sucking everything out.

Willy Whatsthis (24 pages) Anne Montgomery
Children 2–6
Follow the adventures of the coolest toy/companion for any kid whose imagination varies inversely with his net worth. Willy is a found object of indeterminate function and origin but infinite possibilities. Something you might pick up on the side of the road in a bad neighborhood. Willy himself demonstrates his great versatility. ("I'm a gun!" "I'm an assassin's knife!" "I'm a prosthetic limb!" "I'm a robot condom!") We also meet Willy's other friends in the Dumpster Orphanage: Benny Beer Can, Neddie the Needle, and Hazy the Half-Filled Meds Bottle.

A Stitch in Time (420 pages)
Gustav Slocomb
Einstein's Second Theory of Relativity uniquely explained by an absent-minded seamstress. The time/space continuum is explored in terms of garments needing repair. Is "good as new" theoretically possible in a universe where

the speed of light is a constant, but split trousers come in all sizes?

Tollbooths (169 pages)
Earl Slavin
An exhaustive survey of tollbooths from fabled trolls to modern RFID readers. The author includes a special section on how EZ-Pass has made the modern tollbooth so "EZ to forget." The folksy structures of the Merritt Parkway are compared to the "toll plazas" of the Throg's Neck Bridge. Who came up with the idea of the coin basket? Includes interviews with toll takers who share their experiences.

My Private War (310 pages)
Kenneth Delano Abramowitz
A veteran of his own long-term marriage (fifty-two years), Abramowitz shares his marital experiences in excruciating detail. The reader is an eyewitness when the author's rosy-cheeked idealism as a young innocent on the dating circuit is rudely crushed after his first brush with in-laws and the horror of unknown rituals of a spouse in the bathroom.

Driving in the Fog (285 pages)
Alberta Cummins
A Cape Cod mystery set entirely in the backseat of a 1955 Buick. Unable to see their hands in front of their faces because of the fog, the travelers nonetheless set out on

an ill-fated journey that takes them from Scituate to Provincetown…with murder as a rest stop.

Flash Drives: The Whole Story (330 pages)
Victor Kleinmeister, PhD
Those little things we carry around in our pockets know more than they're telling. And to prove it, the author leaves his flash drive in his computer at work over the weekend. When Monday morning comes around, our boy has some 'splainin' to do." Technical data reveals how porn as well as spreadsheets seem to all fit inside.

The Stool (290 pages)
Johnny Dumas
First-time novelist and professional cut man, Dumas tells this classic boxing tale from the point of view of the ubiquitous stool. Brought into the ring at the end of each round or left alone in the gym to ponder the fate of our pugilistic protagonist, this "bottoms up" glimpse into the "sweet science" delivers a knockout punch with the steadfast calm of furniture.

Why Not Prostitution? (160 pages)
Brenda and Serena Williamson
If you've ever thought of becoming a whore, this is your step-by-step guide to breaking into the big time. Qualifying criteria, fees, attributes, grooming tips, and cleanups are all included in this firsthand guide by two professional

veterans of the escort and call-girl circuit. A Vegas pullout is included, along with an Adam's-apple sizing chart.

I Dated My Doorman (230 pages)
Mary McDonough
"He hailed me a cab, and I hailed him" begins this delicious romp of New York apartment living. This first-person narrative recounts the affair that "rocked the co-op board." The author is open and candid about her proclivity for "men in uniform," but she never thought it would happen in her own building. "Now, at Christmastime, he gives *me* a tip," she relates with glee.

The Crimean War and the Recent Housing Crisis (485 pages)
Henry Clay Koppleman
Linking the Crimean War with the present-day housing crisis for the first time, the author relates in detail how both disasters are driven by a sorry lack of leadership and disposable income. Freddie Mac, Fannie Mae, and Barney Frank are all compared to the Charge of the Light Brigade as hopeless causes, no matter what century they're in. All are given equal roles in the demise of life as we know it.

I Was There (350 pages)
Arnold Symington
The author's firsthand account of the currency wars of the 1990s. With unflinching detail, he cites the nickel-and-diming of individuals and companies locked in mortal

monetary combat that often pitted citizens of the same country against one another for the sheer madness of "What's it worth to ya?" and cheap flights.

A Rumor of Money (275 pages)
Marianne Crosley
Passion trumps sensibility in this romance novel, when our heroine overhears that the man she is trying to break up with may be due a huge inheritance. After trying desperately to fall *back* in love with him, she consults Google, D&B, and finally the man's trash can before giving up and letting him go. The surprise ending involves someone younger and much cuter.

The Secret Life of the Rubber Band (305 pages)
Brian Guzman Jacobson
The hitherto lowly rubber band gets the star treatment here with an illustrated journey from factory, to the corner behind your bed—or the floor in front of the mailboxes in your building. Generally vilified and belittled in the United States, the rubber band is used as currency in some countries and as a sexual aid in others.

UNCOUPLING THE CONSCIOUS

"Conscious uncoupling brings wholeness to the spirits of both people who choose to recognize each other as their teacher...If we can allow ourselves this gift, our exoskeleton of protection and imprisonment will fall away and offer us the opportunity to begin constructing an endoskeleton, an internal cathedral, with spiritual trace minerals like self-love, self-acceptance, and self-forgiveness."
—Dr. Habib Sedeghi and Dr. Sherry Sami, as quoted by Natalie Matthews in Elle.com

I am trying to separate my opponent from his intelligence in the third round of a six-rounder at Sunnyside

Gardens. But this particular tomata can ain't goin' down like he should. We' had talked about this. But no, he wants to stay vertical to impress his girlfriend in the second row. I'm thinking, *Conscious uncoupling, that's the ticket.* But this bum is, like, clueless when it comes to conscious uncoupling. In other words, if you know you're going to throw a fight, it should not come as a big surprise when it's time to go. It oughta come as a relief. Uncouple your freakin' conscious, Bozo, and let's get this thing over with.

I hit him with a right cross at the same time he's checking out the girlfriend in the second row. That uncouples his conscious real good. Like, I mean, for real. He goes down like a ton of bricks. Then, when he comes to, suddenly he knows the meaning of "conscious uncoupling." It's gettin' hit so hard you see stars or, even worse, nothin'. You were conscious, then you got uncoupled. And when you wake up, your conscious gets coupled again, but with what, in this case, I don't know. Get over it.

Anyway, I figure that's the business I'm in, the conscious-uncoupling business. I'm a prizefighter. Turned pro fifteen years ago. Never been uncoupled myself, conscious or otherwise. Not even once. I got losses, but none of them by knockouts. Only decisions. There may be a couple of judges in Wheeling or Wilkes-Barre whose conscious I'd like to uncouple, but that's another story.

So when Gwyneth Paltrow says she wants to "conscious uncouple" her half-a-fag husband, I'm thinkin', *What is this, domestic violence?* She doesn't seem the type. Neither one of them could make a fist, if you ask me. But then again, maybe it would be a good thing. Put both of them in a ring and let them go at it. Each tryin' to uncouple the other's consciousness. But wait a second. The girl's a movie star. She'll be doing *Shakespeare in Traction* if things don't go her way. Him, he'll have to change the name of his band to "Coldcocked."

I think "cold cock" is grounds in the UK.

I got a big "conscious uncoupling"—otherwise known as a fight—coming up next month. So right now I'm in training. I got a sparring partner that who comes to me already a little consciously uncoupled, if you know what I mean. The guy's well-meaning, but a real empty suit—or, in his case, trunks. He's about as easy to uncouple as the clasp on a sixteen-year-old's bra. I'll move around with the guy, but I won't hit him with anything. Otherwise, the next thing you know, I'll have an NFL lawsuit on my hands. They got more conscious uncoupling goin' on over there than you could shake a stick at.

Anyway, everybody's makin' a big deal outta Gwyneth and her uncoupling. As if "conscious" makes it feel better. But it all hurts. You go to a doctor and tell him you had a little conscious uncoupling over the weekend, and he orders up an MRI faster than you can say, "Affordable Care Act." They take that stuff seriously. But in the ring, the ref just asks you how many fingers you see, and that's it. I always lie. I always say, "Four." I don't want to get into a big discussion with the guy over whether the thumb is a finger, strictly speaking. It's only got one knuckle.

But when we spar, no one's supposed to be tryin' to uncouple nuttin'. We're sparring. Movin' around. But this guy, he sees it as an opportunity. He starts hittin' me like he's tryin' to uncouple somethin' conscious on me. Then I gotta protect myself at all times, like the ref says. That's how a melee starts. Fight fans love it, but it's real rough on the participants. So if Paltrow was my fighter, I'd tell her, "Don't go for the conscious uncoupling right off the bat, especially if you got a PTA meetin' in the morning."

They say gettin' your conscious uncoupled, like in one shot, is much healthier than takin' a beatin' for a few rounds. I have personally experienced this. Then again, sparring daily with an opponent of any kind can take its toll on you, too. And boxin's even tougher than a long-term marriage, if you can believe it. But with a sparring partner, even though the guy's on your payroll, that kind of uncoupling punishment builds up, and the conscious angle is just part of it. The next thing you know, you're completely consciously uncoupled, sittin' on a stool somewhere crying for no reason at all, or blinkin' your eyes and swivelin' your head around like a puppet. Around the gym, and even on the street, we call that "punch drunk." There's a neurological term for that, but it escapes me at the moment. Hey, wait a second, for all I know, maybe my conscious ain't so coupled no more. What're all them flies doin' in here? Somebody ring a bell. I could use a standin' eight.

So when Paltrow says she's "conscious uncoupling," I don't know what the hell she's talkin' about. She oughta stick to acting and let the mooks like me take care of conscious uncoupling and all that. I'm good at it. She's good at organic food and natural fibers. On the other hand, if she *really* wants to get into the fight game, she'd be a big draw. Sell a lot of tickets. The other guy, I don't know. I seen him skip once, at the Grammys. But with no rope, if you get my drift.

I gotta go. I gotta get back to training for this big conscious-uncoupling thing I got comin' up next month. Hey, somebody close a window. There are flies in here.

IMMEDIATE MILITARY CHANGES NOW THAT "DON'T ASK/DON'T TELL" HAS BEEN REPEALED

- Tanks now named after famous lesbians
- Operation "Fabulous"
- Barbra Streisand's picture on warplanes
- No more "March to the rear"
- Show tunes rather than Sousa marches
- All mention of the term *privates* abolished
- Rank of "rear admiral" suspended

- Instead of medals, Acts of Valor rewarded with "accessories"
- Three-day passes tolerated between consenting soldiers
- Brazilian waxing replaces waterboarding
- All drill teams stripped to the waist
- Chippendale dancers designated "Seal Team 7"
- "Omigod" replaces "Shock and awe"
- Camouflage replaced by "something in a floral print"
- "Hail to the Chief" now played only for the Indian in the Village People
- K rations replaced by KY rations
- Rank of *Specialist* for hair and makeup
- Purple Hearts awarded for "helmet hair"
- Decorators included in first wave of all amphibious landings
- Hugs instead of salutes
- "Semper Fi" is now "Semper Fifi"
- Recruiting centers now issue "casting calls"
- "High and tight" not just for haircuts
- Marines forced to explain that "Chesty Puller" is not the name of a gay porn star
- "The few, the proud, the nelly"
- *Top Gun* now just *Top*
- A close formation is no longer a committed one
- "Hut 2-3-4" replaced by "5-6-7-8"
- Basic training includes jazz, ballet, and tap
- The "Silent Service" is your business

- Out: combat boots. In: tap shoes
- "War is hell" but "Musicals are fabulous"
- "Department of Defense" replaced by "The Drama Department"
- All army training films to start with an episode of *Glee*
- Bomb-sniffing dogs used only to ferret out bad scripts
- Judy Garland awarded posthumous Medal of Honor
- No more "snipers," just great "dish"
- "Joint Chiefs" now "All the Chiefs Together"
- Pilots admonished for making "low passes"
- Orders to "Move out" issued only when there are irreconcilable differences

INDIVIDUALS ON MY GOVERNMENT-SHUTDOWN FURLOUGH LIST

- The announcers in the subway and on Metro North trains. It was better when they were unintelligible.
- The lady who insists on telling me exactly how to leave a message on an answering machine, and then adds "to leave a callback number" just when I think she's finished.
- People riding those Citi Bikes. They look foolish and out of place, and they make me feel guilty and stupid for never having figured the system out.

- Anyone who takes a photograph with a cell phone. It just doesn't look right. It turns everyone into an amateur.
- Miley Cyrus's new teeth. I liked her better when she had gums. Now her mouth looks like a Buick.
- Lottery players ahead of me at the newsstand, when all I want to do is pay for my newspaper.
- The lady who keeps calling me about serious problems with my credit card even though she says everything is perfectly fine.
- Subway dispatchers who are always "holding" the train you're on. Have they ever tried *dispatching* the train instead?
- Animal-shelter personnel who make adopting a cat like trying to get into the Racquet Club. And guess what happens to the poor animal when they blackball you as an unfit owner?
- Taxi drivers who have bad credit-card equipment; or tricky, unfamiliar card swipers that don't work. I don't *want* to "just swipe it again."
- Preschool teachers who make you sit in kindergarten chairs to discuss serious issues about your kid when *they* always grab a normal chair.
- Pet-store owners who insist on clever puns as names for their establishments.
- Charming, articulate subway beggars with better shoes than you.

- Gloria Allred. How does *every* woman with a beef end up with her?
- Complete strangers who say "Bless you" when you sneeze. You have to thank them and make a new friend.
- Television financial analysts. They never have days when they're completely stumped, and they never have to admit they were wrong.
- Marathoners. It's not just the marathon, but they talk about the months of training as well.
- Burger joints that put a whole leaf of lettuce on your burger. It's like eating a drape.
- My cleaning lady, who insists on rearranging the medicine bottles and the toiletries on my sink. Where is my toothbrush *now*?
- My dentist, who thinks he's a comedian. Patch Adams, go fuck yourself.
- Same-sex engagement pictures in the *New York Times*. I know, I know. But do they have to look happier about their gay marriage than I was about my straight one?
- Toys for Tots. Lemme get this straight. The brave soldiers of our US Marines take all those toys and personally distribute them while defending our country? Hoooorah!
- Hamid Karzai. You're at war, fuckface. Stop wearing your jacket over your shoulders like a movie Nazi or metrosexual.

MY POT NOT SO LUCKY

"*The invitation was to a potluck. Guests were meant to bring food inspired by (Nora) Ephron's career or by the woman herself.*"
—Sam Sifton, in the *New York Times Magazine*

My wife decided to have a little potluck dinner for my birthday. She thought it would be cute if she told everyone to bring a dish that, in some way, had been inspired by my career, or even by just me, myself. She wanted to celebrate my life and accomplishments in the same way Nora Ephron had been celebrated for hers at *her* potluck dinner. I was dubious. My wife insisted it would be wildly sophisticated and ever so much fun.

Then the big day arrived. I was joined at the dinner table by family, friends, so-called friends, and a couple of characters I didn't know at all, and was, honestly, afraid to have in my house, much less share a meal with.

Edna Tomosulo started off the evening with some specially prepared hors d'oeuvres. They consisted of crackers to commemorate my brief stint at the Parchman Farm state-prison facility in Mississippi on a trumped-up charge of grand theft auto after college. I had almost succeeded in finally putting that sorry event behind me and had gotten on with my life, but the crackers brought me abruptly back. Edna delightedly pointed out that her hors d'oeuvres were served with dabs of bitter herbs on them, reminiscent of my first marriage to that borderline bitch who took my money and my self-esteem. The herbs were then smeared with stewed kidney pâté to mark the fact that she'd also left the marriage with one of my renal organs, which I had donated to her in a desperate effort to save her life and our marriage. It turned out she was faking both and just wanted to see if I would do it.

Then Ursula Cieplinski thought it would be cute to contribute some blood sausage on toothpicks as a tribute to what happened to my dick the time I inadvertently slammed it in her car door when we were briefly dating. Fortunately, I was drunk at the time and thought there was something wrong with the door, so I repeatedly tried to slam it shut even harder, but then it occurred to me that, hey, wait a second, maybe that new trumpet I hadn't finished paying for but insisted on bringing to the party was causing the problem. So you can imagine my relief when that sharp, shooting pain turned out to be only my cock and not my Selmer, which I subsequently returned to Manny's. Boy, was my face red when I got home and sobered up. Almost as red as my penis. I then took myself to the ER and was treated by an intern I'd gone to school with. He fixed me up and said nothing. The blood sausage was a nice touch, but swallowing it and remembering, at the same time, the incident it represented made me queasy.

Pigs in a blanket were produced by Sue Kiley, of which she'd been a prime example when I'd shown up at the Killington ski resort with a friend known as "the Human Tick" in a van fitted out with mattresses in the back, along with Sue and another friend of questionable beauty from North Adams State Teacher's College. The ladies had remained naked, prone, and wrapped in the same comforter for the entire weekend. Police had been called, and my reputation as a youth counselor was ruined in the process.

When we finally sat down, Chet LaRoche served up a large bowl of squash, recalling the flattened state of any hopes I'd ever had of becoming a jazz musician or a Green Beret. Chet pointed out the subtle garnish of nuts to signify the fact that I'd been deemed psychologically unfit to even think I could do either. Suddenly, I was thrust back to the summer of 1961 when I had tried to enlist. I was home after leaving college under dubious circumstances, which included sleeping with the local liquor store owner's wife, an inability to decide between spaghetti sauces at the grocery store, and my failure to go to class.

Albert Brannigan contributed popovers as a nod to my lifelong battle with premature ejaculation, which I suffered even as a toddler.

Blackened carp celebrated the beating I'd sustained as a result of criticizing the length of an ironworker's mullet during the construction of the first World Trade Center. I had been on a bicycle at the time.

I began to moan as I dug into my cheese twists brought by Anna Tumadowski, marking the time I had badly sprained my ankle doing a "Gene Kelly" on the wall of an apartment building lobby trying to win the affections of, and gain access to, a girl who was neither impressed by my grand jeté nor moved by the injury I sustained on her behalf.

Baked Alaska was served, reminiscent of my infatuation with Sarah Palin's hair as a sexual talisman. I knew then I had been too vocal about my desire to touch it with my nose.

People seemed to be having a jolly time at the dinner, but I found that my mood was becoming anything but celebratory. Sadness and doom were creeping over me like nail fungus.

The Churchill twins brought beef jerky and pulled pork to remind the assembled that I' had been disciplined at prep school for masturbating with an Electrolux.

Ladyfingers from my younger brother were meant to celebrate the fact that I preferred rectal exams by female urologists because of their slender digits, as compared to the fat fingers of the male doctor and Holocaust survivor who had been intent on treating my chronic prostatitis in Beverly Hills with massage, saying in broken Viennese every time he withdrew his gloved hand, *"Ubi pus, ibi evacua."*

A selection of sour grapes was brought by Clark Johnson and others to represent my feelings about the fact that I'd never been elected president of anything at any point in my career, or in any class or organization I'd ever been part of—even after specifically asking to be chosen, and embarrassing myself by actively campaigning. It became my equivalent of Red Buttons's "Never had a dinner" lament. I never had a dinner, either, except this potluck one, and I was becoming less and less sure about whether I was feeling honored.

Because of my lackluster record of leadership or executive abilities, not one guest opted to bring Imperial margarine, Red Chief tomatoes, Commander lettuce, or even chicken a la king. But several guests showed up with plenty of Hamburger Helper, cold fish, rump roast, twice-baked potatoes, and an assortment of paillards, none of which I took as a compliment.

Then a large bowl of cornballs appeared, supplied by Mitzi Bruce, who remembered my debut/finale as a stand-up comic at the Bitter End, where the audience, trying desperately to help by laughing, simply could not decipher the appropriate time or place to do it. In desperation, my act devolved from ersatz Woody Allen to bad Marty Allen. Then, in a last-ditch effort to elicit any response, I closed with a passable impression of Ed Sullivan—itself lifted from the trombone player in *The Tonight Show* band. In the impression, Ed is receiving a blow job from his beloved wife, Sylvia, while sitting on the toilet. "Right here on my cock." (*Cock* being a great Ed Sullivan word, like *pistachio* or *radicchio*.) "Y'know, Sylvia, this is a fine, fine blow job you're giving me right here in this really big bathroom." Cornballs, indeed.

My wife herself served up some Rocky Road ice cream for dessert to go with the rhubarb birthday cake. Everyone who knew our marriage intimately was thrilled by the appropriateness.

The rhubarb birthday cake had a glaze on top instead of frosting to represent my empty stare as of late. But it also meant that the potluck commemoration was right up to the minute.

I rose to thank everyone and give my toast. I named every dish that had been supplied by the guests, and in the order they'd been presented. Then I excused myself, went to the bathroom by the front door, and promptly threw them all up in reverse order. There, driving the porcelain bus (or "reading Crane" as we used to say in college), my life literally flashed before me and into the toilet bowl. From "glazed" through "scrambled," sour grapes followed by cornballs, right down to a "dip" of unknown origin—I returned from whence I had come.

But then a latecomer, Horace Cowper, arrived, and everyone had to sit down again to feast on his offering of turkey hash commemorating the only play of mine that had been semi produced. *HamToLet* had failed miserably to the schadenfreude of all my friends assembled at the birthday dinner. Thus, the turkey hash seemed perfectly suited for the evening. There followed a critical discussion of *HamToLet*, which was a modern reworking of *Hamlet* as the perverse "butcher of Denmark," who insisted on renting meat rather than selling it. It was a vain attempt to marry Shakespeare and *Porky's*.

Oh, how they laughed at the dialogue at the end of act one when "Ohfeelya," after having been ravaged in a hayloft by the butcher, turns to the audience and says plaintively, "Is this a stable relationship?" (Curtain) The play closed in tech rehearsal and was simultaneously shut down by the health department. I always took it as a triumph that it had been produced at all. But apparently, my good friends, with their droll foodstuffs, felt differently.

The evening finally ended. All my friends took their platters, bowls, baskets, and bags that the potluck dishes had come in and promptly left.

I turned to my wife. "What was that all about?" I asked.
"Your life," she said.
"My life? That was my life?"
"Potluck." She smiled.

OH, MAMA!

You won't find a happier guy than me when she finally makes it. It's what she wanted all along, and I supported her 1,000 percent. Hey, I helped her get there, so why wouldn't I be pleased as punch? We're talking sainthood here. The big one. A *saint*. Forever. The religious kind—not like she just got drafted by New Orleans.

When I knew her, it wasn't the white *schmattas* with the blue trim. That came later. It was pink and green all the way. And pearls. That was it. She had a line of credit at Talbots. I never saw the flip-flops, or whatever she was wearing toward the end. When we were together, it was only properly broken-in Topsiders. Never Bass Weejuns. That was for preppy poseurs, she always said.

God, I loved her. But so did God. How do you like *that* for a three-way?

Anyway, I was an instructor at the Bel Air Yacht Club, and the first time I laid eyes on Terry, she wheeled into the parking lot in a Morgan, for crissakes. (Oops, sorry. The three-way thing is still a little raw with me.) A Morgan! Canvas top detached, leather bonnet belt, British racing green. She looked great—and so did Terry.

And then she did that thing that all great women know how to do from birth. She pushed her aviators up on her head where her hair band usually was, and they stayed there for the rest of the day. Sandy-blond hair, white straight teeth (she really should have looked after herself more after the move to Calcutta). In those days, it was a Mitzi Gaynor look or maybe Debbie Reynolds before Eddie. OK, Terry Moore, but at her *peak*. All sporty and all girl. She looked like she was born to be on the bow of a Lightning with her hand cupped to her mouth, yelling at some loser barging the starting line and being photographed for a spread in *Life* magazine at the same time.

You see, saints aren't born. They're made. And I'm not talking the way you're thinking, even if I *was* the first. Terry became "saintly" only *after* her junior year abroad in Calcutta. I remember lying with her on the beach at the country club that Fourth of July, saying, "C'mon, Ter, *Calcutta?* What the *hell?* I thought Wheaton girls went to Florence to study Renaissance painting and architecture."

Everything's Wront

Fourth of July on that beach with Terry was when we consummated our relationship. I mean, this was the early '60s, *before* the pill and computer dating. There wasn't a lot of sex then, just dry humping and impossible bra clasps. So when actual full-metal sex happened, you *deserved* rockets and sparklers. That's when I realized I might lose her. Jesus was definitely on her mind even then. I heard it with my own ears, but being young and in love, I chose not to notice or take it personally. But looking back on that night, *He* was *definitely* in the picture. Big time. OK, maybe not, "*sainthood* big time" yet, but He was around. *A lot.*

That summer with Terry was the best time of my life. She taught the beginner sailors (she was great with the kids), and I taught intermediate and advanced. She was in Blue Jays; I was in Lightnings. And together we were in heaven. Well, OK, not where she is today. But it was still pretty good. C'mon, it was Greenwich, and life was sweet.

She would always ask, "Where is this relationship going?" which is what she probably said, I'm sure, to Jesus when the time came. God only knows what she meant by it. I told her I eventually wanted to marry her. I couldn't imagine life without her. I was graduating that year from Williams and was already working at Armstrong Cork, so a little wifey-poo would fit right into the picture. We'd skip New York, Terry and me, and move right to Rowayton or maybe New Canaan (except I hate that commute and those architect assholes up there) and have kids. I told her we'd name the first one Morgan after her car.

Toward Labor Day when she was getting ready to shove off to Calcutta on the *Rotterdam*, a half-assed Holland America ship if there ever was one, with designer *luggage* if you can believe it, things changed. This wasn't going to be any hippie trip to India. She was way beyond that. I don't think she even knew what a sari was back then. But, toward Labor Day I felt her pulling away. The lovemaking was still nonstop. (Hey, we were young—that's all I could think about.) I think we did it thirty-seven days straight and in every room of the house on Round Hill Road where she was staying for the summer. She was uninhibited like crazy, but afterward, smoking cigarettes in the master bedroom, she would grow silent and sullen. Then she would get out of bed and sit at the lady-of-the-house's dressing table and try on all her makeup. She had a thing about her lips. She thought they were too thin, and this was way before collagen or Barbara Hershey. She would sit there at the lady's dressing table, balls-ass naked with those breasts that you could get into art school with just by drawing them. And with the powder puff resting on her cheek, she'd look into the mirror and say, "I wish I were dead."

It was then that I knew she was headed for a life that didn't include me. It was Him again. She didn't even try to hide it anymore and would talk about Jesus freely and openly and especially whenever she had a really big orgasm.

And then she left for the junior year abroad that never ended. I had the feeling I would never see her again when

I said good-bye to her in her stateroom before she sailed. We made love one last time. The sex was smokin' hot because it was like being on a train but without the wheels. And get this. You know why it was the best? Because just as she climaxed and arched her back like Nadia Comaneci, the ship's horn blew one of those long, low, throaty blasts, and it drowned out the whole "Jesus, I'm coming *again*" nonsense; and for those few brief seconds, those last seconds together as lovers, I felt we were at last alone. Thank you, Jesus, for not sharing.

I left the boat with a tear in my eye. As I walked down the gangplank, I thought, *Terry's such a free spirit, she'll probably find someone else by the time the ship clears Ambrose. And they'll do it in the lifeboats under the canvas just like we would if I were onboard. Ha-ha. Big deal.*

The rest is history. She stayed in Calcutta, and to tell you the truth, in my opinion she really let herself go. I always wondered what happened to that Morgan. It'd be worth a million today. Talk about feeding the hungry!

When I hear people say, "Mother Teresa this" and "Mother Teresa that," I always tell them, "I used to go with her." But then I always add, so they know I'm not bitter or strange about it, "Hey, if I hadn't broken up with her, *I'd* be up for sainthood." That always gets a laugh, although I wouldn't want to go through what she had to go through to get there.

Once in India, she started hanging out with a different crowd, the sick and dying, and that was it. But she would always take my calls in the early days after she got famous with the dying people—and after the Nobel. "*Sweeeeeeeetie!*" she'd say into the phone sounding like her old self on Long Island Sound. "How *are* you? I *miss* you. How're the boys?" She always asked after the kids, which I felt bad about because Jesus didn't want any more kids, and she never had any. But to tell you the truth, I always wondered why she never threw me or any of her old friends a bone or anything. I mean, she had Jesus's ear. She could've set someone up with the snap of a finger. And we could've helped the Big Guy. Marketing, morality, peace, hunger, whatever. But maybe He's the jealous type. Guys like Him usually are. They don't want to know their ladies have ever been with anyone else. Anyway, I stopped calling after a while, and she never called *me* except once when she needed some lines for an award she was getting. Apparently, I was good enough for a freebie but not for a paying gig like, maybe, cardinal. But still, people would point to me whenever Jesus's name came up and the special "arrangement" He had with her, and they'd say, "Mother Teresa used to be his girlfriend," but it never got me anywhere.

Hey, she found what she was looking for. The Other Guy won. My hat's off to Him. He's a better man than me. Of course, being the Son of God helps. But what the hell. You can't fight City Hall. And look, it paid off. We make our beds and we lie in them, and sometimes we never get up. She didn't have to let herself go like that. But, hey, maybe that's the way Jesus likes her.

OSAMA BIN LADEN'S DIARY

March 23, 2005
First day in the new digs. Each wife wanted to be carried over the threshold. Come on, Allah! Number 4 felt like a boatload of AK-47s. She's history. I only built this place because they thought our last hideout was "Tora *Boring*!"

April 2, 2005
We're staying on the top floor. I would have a nice view if there were *windows*. I left a perfectly nice cave for this? Just found out that there's no cable, no Internet, no phone. Death to America! I have to vote on *Idol* by courier. And then it's too late. Don't know if Clay Aiken is blonde, brunette, or even straight anymore.

January 27, 2005
Pretty much settled in. I tell the wives only one of them on the third floor at a time. They're already going a little stir-crazy. I can't keep them off Home Shopping Network. Am I the only one who thinks the new "Snuggie" looks promising? Much more comfortable than the "Slanket." And "one size fits all terrorists". So I ordered one. By courier. The shipping and handling are gonna kill me.

November 10, 2006
The summer was a nightmare. Why do I have nineteen children? I could have had sex with the Octomom twice and been done with it. One of my teenagers wanted to know if Susan Boyle died, would she be one of the seventy-two virgins. I told him only if Allah is an American. Otherwise the Boyle girl will live forever on this earth.

February 3, 2007
I have seen videos of me. I think this Snuggie makes me look fat *and* evil. I know it sounds like a cliché, but my wives don't understand me. Number 3 gave me a Brazilian yesterday because I refused to dye my pubic hair to match my beard. Now I look like a jihadist on top and Howie Mandel on the bottom.

July 30, 2010
I have not been outside in four years. I am the most wanted man in the world, and Pauly D from the *Jersey Shore* has a

better tan. Wife Number 1 thinks she looks like Snookie. I say, "Maybe your *armpit*. Does the word *shave* mean anything to you?" We fight all the time. So I have to repeat the exact same jihad three times a day. It's worse than being held over at the Villa Roma. Yesterday, Number 2 called my seventy-two virgins, Allah willing, "those frigid bitches from hell." Now I know my life is *really* in danger.

December 16, 2010
I am going out of my skull. Last night I was watching that no-talent Khalid Sheikh Mohammed on the television and shot the picture tube out with my AK-47. Now Number 1 calls me "Al Qaeda Elvis." Numbers 2 and 3 have been bugging me to take them somewhere. I said, "How 'bout the second floor?" They say Abbottabad was never as funny as Costellobad. That's where *they* wanted to build.

February 28, 2011
This is not working out. I am forced to resort to an elixir to regain my sexual potency—except for Wife Number 1. She's only twenty-nine and often wears push-up "Wonderburqas." But for all the others, I almost require Viagra dialysis. My courier can't get a prescription, so he brings me a bottle of cheap herbal camel coaxer instead. Charlie Sheen does not have these problems. He has goddesses. I have wives who get crank calls delivered on flash by men with goats. I should be more like Charlie Sheen. "Jihadding!"

March 9, 2011

I finally got some *real* Viagra. Don't ask where, but I found a doctor in Canada who would write prescriptions for infidels on the Internet. It hasn't done much for my sex life, but at least I always have a place to hang my turban and never fall out of bed anymore. As it is, the remote is still the hardest thing I've had in my hand in years. This morning, the youngest wife said that lying down with me was like having sex with a drone. The most hated man in the world is not a drone. Perhaps, if I stuck my Predator up her burqa, it would teach her a lesson. I can only get pornography by courier, but it is very old by the time it arrives. The last one starred Betty White. And the only thing she took off was her shoes. That's OK. It *still* worked.

April 27, 2011

My stash of porn is exceedingly lame. Does the courier not know that two humps do not a sexy camel make? My idiot son thinks "booby trap" is a porn title. The most explosive thing he's brought me so far is a USB with something called "Burqa's Gone Wild" on it. It would be nice to see a woman undress and expose something softer than a bomb on her chest. The Snuggie is only good for covering the TV when one of the wives walks in.

May 1, 2011

I am jealous of Gaddafi. He has a large-breasted blonde nurse and female bodyguards and hasn't had to marry even *one* of them. Well, diary, that's all for today. I think I will turn in for the night. What is that? I am hearing something that sounds like, "Wop, wop, wop, wop." Either *Jersey Shore* has an air force, or my Paki friends are making low passes to be funny again. I am hearing a crash. My teenage sons must be sucking on too many hookahs...and also *smoking* too much as well. Wait. I hear heavy breathing and the sound of seals barking. People in combat boots are coming up the stairs. Ah, praise Allah, it can only mean that, tonight, all *three* wives want me at one time...I will take two Viagra and insist they do a pole dance. On me! I can hear them at the bedroom door. Good night, dear diary...Honeys, please come in...I'm ready for you...

SELFIES

I'm a selfie stylist. A lot of people want to do selfies, but they really don't have the chops. That's where I come in. Say you want to do a selfie but your life sucks. You call me. I come over with a nightclub backdrop or a Bieber-concert thingamabob, and, bam, you've got yourself a selfie you can put on the Internet without having people call you a loser.

I also book celebs to "bomb" your selfie. Like, I could get Rob Schneider for a certain amount of money to just "happen" to be walking by in a club (my fake background) or an airport (real) when you want to take a selfie, and that crazy guy bombs your selfie and sticks his head in the frame. What a guy! Thanks, Rob. I'll treasure that moment and this selfie forever.

I had nothing to do with the president's selfie. You could tell it was pure amateurville. It was pretty lame. I could have helped him. In fact, if you want to know, the real story was Obama was minding his own business at Mandela's funeral, and the Danish prime minister decided to take a selfie to show her friends back in Copenhagen. That's when the prez, that nut, decided to bomb the PM's selfie. She's from Denmark, so what does she know? She came all the way down for the funeral, but in South Africa, good-looking Nordic blondes are a dime a dozen. Figure it out. Apartheid's only been history for twenty years. So she was doing her selfie, and some, like, Danish government hack—not me—tells the president, "Hey, bomb that selfie and I'll give you a trade agreement." Boom, done. Now she goes home and says, "I took a selfie at the Mandela thing. You know, the one with the sign language guy who could've been an actual silent assassin? And guess who bombed my picture? A skinny black guy. Is that a trip?"

The selfie styling business is pretty good. Justin Bieber is a client. He likes to do full hair and makeup for all his selfies. No matter what. Ever notice how his hair is just so? He has that curl working. And he's always got the chin down to accent his lower lip and bring out the baby blues. And his eyes are rolled up just a little so you can see the whites underneath. That's me! I did that.

People ask me why I never take a selfie of myself. Personally, I don't get it. The problem with a selfie is that, well, it's a selfie. Most selfies are taken at a distance of twenty-five inches. Thirty inches, tops. Even *I* can't change that. Now, at twenty-five inches, the face tends to get spread out like a topographical map of Russia, and the nose starts to look like a bulbous mountain of flattened flesh in the middle of your cheeks. And the mouth? Forget about the mouth. Everybody smiles for a selfie. Big mistake. At twenty-five inches, your teeth look like the front end of a 1953 Skylark.

For instance, you never see Kevin Bacon do a selfie. Why? Bad camber with the nose. He hasn't got the nostrils for it. It could put a degree of separation on his career that even *he* couldn't overcome. Kevin Bacon's nose in a selfie would look like the entrance to Carlsbad Caverns. But that doesn't stop most people. Most selfies make a little upturned nose look like a yellow squash. That's why I tell the Biebs to keep his chin down. And me, I never take a selfie. I know better.

But selfies are here to stay, no matter how bad they look without a stylist. If selfies had been around for *all* the presidents, our money would look like Facebook on paper. As it is, no one even wants to sit for a portrait anymore if it's done by someone else. But sit for a selfie? No problem. Gimme that phone. They ought to call it a "cellfie." There wouldn't be selfies without phones. Phones are everything now. I even saw that the word *selfie* made it into the *Oxford*

Dictionary, and that's cool. Very good for my business. But bad for selfies in general. I mean, the president of the United States is doing selfies. But it wasn't his phone, I tell you. You know why I know that? Because you can't take a decent selfie on a Blackberry. It was a hackable smartphone that belonged to the blonde, and Obama was just bombing. Oops.

These days selfies are spreading like, well, like selfies. One police department in Nevada makes inmates take their own mug shots now. They're called "mugsies." One front and one from the side. Although the one from the side doesn't really count as a selfie. Profiles are so snapshot.

But I gotta go. I got a lot of selfies to set up today. No one goes out anymore. They don't have to. Do a selfie with a little help from you know who, and it looks like you're a social butterfly. Whoa! I just nabbed Joy Behar to do a bomb. She needs the work. And she'll only cost you a nickel, but you'll have a memory that'll last a lifetime—if anyone remembers who she was.

I even heard Kim Jong-un's uncle did a selfie when he was being executed recently just to take his mind off his troubles and to show he had a sense of humor. I wonder if he kept his chin down. I know he wasn't smiling.

DON'T TOUCH THAT THROAT, MY FRIEND

Felonious assault rose by 8 percent this year in New York City, but police officials say it's only because strangulation is now considered a felony.

—WNYC Radio news

MEMO
FROM: Vinny Indelicato
TO: Bosses, underbosses, captains, consigliore, made men, crew, associates, friends of ours, wives, goomahs, goombahs, clients, TSA agents, floorwalkers, hall monitors, David Carradine, priests, nuns, and mothers-in-law
SUBJECT: Strangulation

Strangulation is now a felony in New York City.

Wha? It used to be no big deal. A misdemeanor, maybe, tops. C'mon, a little neck music, that's all. Maybe you could get a ticket for it, like a movin' violation—if you did it right. Or else just a warning, if the cop liked the color of your eyes or was feelin' good that day or just didn't want to have to show up in court all day if you tried to beat it. But now? Now strangulation's a freakin' *felony*, for crissakes.

All of a sudden New York's makin' a big freakin' deal outta somethin' that used to work pretty good for us. Now you got your first-degree strangulation and your second-degree strangulation. The only good news is that third-degree strangulation is still only a Class A Misdemeanor. And wearing a shirt with the collar so tight it turns your face red is merely a fashion faux pas.

Before they upgraded this move from a complaint" (as in "If you can't do the clasp without strangling me, I'll do it myself") to a freakin' felony (as in "Arrrrggggghhhhhhhaaah, OK. I'll give ya your stupid money"), most of the reported cases of aggravated neck nonsense were handled by the Parking Authority, the Taxi and Limousine Commission, or whoever it is that does rent control. But now, all of a sudden, we got the police involved with this thing of ours, and they mean it.

As a result, all law-enforcement personnel now gotta receive training in recognizing certain crimes of the neck and knowing exactly when they gotta do somethin' about it and get involved. I mean, you got your "necking" in the backseat of a car, your "rubbernecking" at the scene of an accident, and the ever-present being a general "pain in the neck" around the office or, especially, in a long-term relationship. But who's to say what's a "strangle" and what's a little encouragement to come up with the vig when you finally got the rat bastard by the throat who's been ducking you for weeks on end?

Before this, strangulation was never a felony. Law-enforcement officials, mobsters, and marriage counselors alike always considered it somewhere between a nudge and a nuisance. Generally, excessive squeezing of body parts had always been classified as perfectly acceptable—up to a point. But with the present reclassification, once you get above the shoulders but below the chin, what was once generally considered a turn-on—especially in the persuasion department—is now a turnoff and a big freakin' federal case just because the throat is involved. Apparently, it has something to do with breathing. In other words, a few bad apples have gotten strangulation elevated all the way to a felony instead of being a perfectly normal way of punctuatin' a domestic argument, makin' a political point, or maybe collectin' what is owed to you, or even tryin' to get a waiter's attention at Sardi's.

What I'm sayin' is, if strangulation is suddenly a felony, what's next? Ventilatin' somebody with an ice pick? The next thing you know, you won't be able to throw nobody off a building without the cops goin' crazy. Sittin' on a couch with dirty pants could get you a misdemeanor one day. Or blowing your nose with no tissue, one nostril at a time—you could get a ticket for that, or maybe two.

Our way of life is being threatened by this action. And now they're worried sick about crime statistics spikin' on account of it. It's their fault. It's like makin' stealin' a kiss grand-theft larceny. The world is changing, my friends. And if everyone's gonna be a freakin' convicted felon from now on, who's gonna vote Republican?

SUICIDE BOMBING 101

A commander at a secluded terrorist training camp north of Baghdad unwittingly used a belt packed with explosives while conducting a demonstration early Monday for a group of militants, killing himself and twenty-one others.

—The *New York Times*

A police officer said the camp members were attending a lesson on making car bombs and explosive belts when a glitch set off one of the devices.

—The *New York Post*

Good morning, everyone. My name is Professor Abdul Nassim Madawi, and I will be teaching Suicide

Bombing 101 this semester. This is a noncore curriculum course, but while it will count toward your overall credits for graduation, it cannot be used as a prerequisite for your major. You cannot graduate using this course. Let me put it this way. If you graduate after taking this course, you flunk. Understood? OK. Let's get started. Here is a syllabus of what this course will cover. Please take one and pass it on.

A) Suicide Bombing: Vest or Belt?
   1) Picking Out the Right One
   2) Fashion Counts
      a) Be a Bomber, Don't Look Like One
      b) Does This Suicide Vest Make Me Look Fat?
         i. Is Durability an Issue?
         ii. "Dress for Success!"
         iii. Burqa Dos and Don'ts

B) The IED
   1) What Is an Improvised Explosive Device?
      a) DIY or "Store Bought"
   2) What If I'm No Good at Improvisation?
   3) Is Fallujah Iraq's *Second City*?
      a) Taking Suggestions from Snipers
      b) Saying "Yes and" with Explosives
         i. Listen!
         ii. Don't Block
         iii. Have Fun

C) Targets
  1) Getting There
     a) Is Public Transportation a Dead Giveaway?
     b) Declining Insurance on a Rental
  2) No Smoking
  3) Scenic Route or Direct?
  4) What You'll Need
     a) "The Ugly Suicide Bomber"
     b) You're Not in the Classroom Anymore

D) Exams, Tests, and Quizzes
  1) What Will Be on the Final?
  2) What to Expect in a Pop Quiz
     a) The Element of Surprise
  3) Pulling an "All-Nighter"
     a) Pass-Fail
  4) Graduation
     a) Virginity Testing

OK. Let's get started. I assume that all of you signed up for this course because you all want to be suicide bombers. I hope no one here is taking this course just for the credit. Don't waste my time. I'm going to assume you're serious. And that's the way I'm going to teach this class. If you're not serious, then, please, you really ought to transfer out right now to public speaking, or maybe something in the music department. If all you're looking for is just a credit, this is not a gut course. In fact, I like to tell my students that suicide bombing is a *guts* course. Think about it. On the other hand, the good news is that if you take this course, you don't have to worry about any of your other courses or final exams or even graduation. If you pass this course, your troubles are over.

Now, what is a suicide bomber? Or, more correctly, *who* is a suicide bomber? It's a guy or a gal who wants to learn something that he or she can use in the future. Presumably the very *near* future. They want to learn something that will make a difference, something they can take with them when they leave here. The takeaway from this course is enormous. It's a skill; it's a way of life. It's even an art form.

The first thing you have to learn about is the vest. Something like this baby right here. Don't worry. It's OK. It's not live. I know what I'm doing. But this is where it all begins and ends: the wearing of the vest. This is what you're working toward, and what your parents paid their hard-earned tuition money for. This is a suicide vest. But it's not a vest like you've ever seen or worn before. In fact, sometimes it's just a belt. And don't worry. I'll let you try on both at the end of the class.

But first of all, why do we call it a vest when, clearly, it doesn't really look like any vest you, or even a Western infidel, has ever worn? That's because right here, here, here, and back here are pockets that are filled with explosives. Don't worry. These are just fake charges. If these were real, you wouldn't be sitting there for very long.

And sometimes it isn't even a vest at all, but merely a belt-type apparatus specially made to hold explosives. But in this course, we're only going to concentrate on the vest as an article of clothing *and* a weapon of choice. Frankly, the belt thing is pretty rudimentary and primitive. So, in this course, I teach the vest, which is pretty much the standard worldwide.

OK. Now I'm going to put this sucker on so you can see how it looks. At the end of the class, you can try it on, too, so you can get the feel of the real thing. If this were a real suicide vest, loaded and ready to go, it would be wired to a trigger such as this, which would then be threaded through the pant leg and into my pocket. Now, some prefer the cell-phone detonator, but I feel that's more technology than we really need, unless a handler is involved and intends to trigger the device from a distance. But then that wouldn't be, strictly speaking, a suicide bomber, now would it?

Am I going too fast? Fine. I'll wait while you catch up on your notes. By the way, a trigger and a detonator are the same thing. So don't worry. That won't be a trick question on the test. All right, then. If we're all caught up, I have my suicide vest on now, and everything is in place. Now, if I were on assignment, of course, this would all be covered with normal clothing. You can't go around wearing one of these on the *outside* of your jacket or burqa. Then, I would simply walk up to a group of people, such as you sitting right here in this class. Don't worry. Nothing's loaded. These explosives aren't real. They're just for teaching purposes.

I would walk up to a group of people as if I were one of them or going to join them or ask them a question. Basically, the trick is to meld into the crowd so that no one notices you're there. That's why wardrobe is so important. I mean, you can imagine what it would be like if I wore this thing on the *outside* and in the open. People would scatter immediately. You don't want that.

But then, when I think the time is right, and I've sort of disappeared into whatever crowd I've chosen—in this case, you students—then, very calmly, I would just flip the trigger switch in my pocket like—

TRUMP CAMPAIGN BUMPER STICKERS

- Vote for Trump
- Trump for Trump
- Melaniamania
- Why Vote When You Can Trump?
- Give Me Trump or Give Me Everything
- I Trump
- Me!
- Hair You Can Believe In
- Hair Today, Prosperity Tomorrow
- If the Comb-over Don't Fit, Fuhgeddaboudit
- Pout This!

- I Do, I Do, I Do
- The Trump Wall Is for the Kool-Aid Man, Too
- Trumpica the Beautiful
- Star-Spangled Trump
- A Comb-over on Every Head
- You're Trump Till Trump Says I Love Trump
- Don't Be a Wimp, Vote for Trump
- Trumpamemnon
- Trumpettes for Trump
- Trump Hair *Do*
- Trump, the President
- United States of Trump
- Put Trump in the Trump House
- Trumping in America
- Give America a Good Trumping
- "Trump, Trump, Trump," the Boys Are Marching
- I Hump Trump
- No More Apprentice
- I Thunka Trump
- Triple or Nothing
- A Trump in Time Could Save This Fucking Country
- Stump with Trump
- I'm Rich
- Millions You Can Believe In
- I'll Find Obama and Take *Him* Out
- Our Future Is Trump, Not Rosie
- I Like Trump
- Trump *I* Can Believe In

- With Liberty and Justice for Trump
- For a Good Time, Call Lindsay Graham
- The Hair's the Thing
- Go Trump Yourself
- Me Again!
- Did I Say Trump?
- Ivana, Ivanka & Trumpy, Too
- Set Your Hair on Fire with Trump
- Dominate with Trump
- Give Me Trump or Give Me Trump
- I Have Not Yet Begun to Trump
- Don't Give Up the Trump
- Cling to the Trump
- Did I Say I'm Rich?
- Put My Money Where Your Vote Is
- I'll Buy Your Vote
- I Want *You* to Roll Over
- Money, Money, Money
- Had Any Trump Lately?
- Have It Trump's Way
- You Deserve a Trump Today
- Trump Me Once and Trump Me Twice and, Fuck It, Trump Me Once Again
- Real Trump
- A Trump among Men
- The Real Thing's the Real Trump
- If You Haven't Anything Trump to Say, Don't Say Anything at All

- Trumpin' in the Mornin', Trumpin' in the Evenin', Trumpin' in the Summertime
- I've Got a Feeling I'm Trump
- 2016 Trumpolympics
- It's Only Trump
- Don't Trump Till You See the Whites of Their Eyes
- Show Me the Trump
- Money Can't Buy You Happiness, but Trump Can
- Better Than Viagra
- Purell in Every Pot
- Hair Apparently
- Only Trump Will Tell
- A Trump in Time Saves Nine
- The Only Trump We Have to Trump Is Trump Itself
- It's Trump Time
- You Lookin' at Trump?
- Trump or Nothin'
- Seal It with a Trump
- It's Not a Vote Until I Say It's a Vote
- You're Voted
- Get Fired Up
- The First President to Move into a Smaller House
- I've Never Been More Serious in My Life
- Elect Me and I'll Prove I'm Electable
- From the Boardroom to the War Room
- "Comb" Over to Trump
- The Best Things in Life Are Trump
- Trump I Can

- The Audacity of Trump
- What, Me Trump?
- Vote Trump Till It Hurts
- Vote for the One with the Fringe on Top

WATCHFUL WHAT?

SUMMARY

Current treatments for prostate cancer include traditional open surgery, robotic surgery, partial prostatectomy, radiation, proton beam, radioactive seed implantation, ultrasound, diet, hyper ejaculation, hookers, surrogates, anal intercourse, and a sharp stick. But recent studies indicate the more efficient course of treatment is "watchful waiting" or "benign neglect." This paper proposes an alternate noninvasive procedure that achieves the same results as all the above: "indifferent disdain," best achieved through a long-term marriage.

ABSTRACT

"Indifferent disdain" has been known to shrink the male prostate to about the size of a pea in a relatively short period of time. Whereas "watchful waiting" assumes a normal sex life, "indifferent disdain" ensures the complete lack of any sexual activity with a wife, girlfriend, life partner, or even, in extreme cases, with Bree Olson and a laptop.

Administered by a domestic partner, "indifferent disdain" takes the form of scowls, winces, frowns, pantomimed projectile vomiting, reenactment of self-induced oral evacuation by the placement of the forefinger near or on the uvula of the throat, abrupt changes of subject, storm-outs, the slamming down of eating utensils, the loud closing of interior doors, rollovers, cold shoulders, feigned distraction, feigned sleep, feigned loss of hearing, feigned state of *stunnade*, slammed car doors, abrupt braking and unscheduled stops, cries of disgust, indications of shock and/or panic, pre-rape horror, impressions of Munch's *The Scream*, derisive put-downs, condescending smirks, patronizing pats, or blank stares. The resultant reduction in the size of the prostate and surrounding sexual and erectile tissue and glands is immediately achieved and, over a relatively short period of time, becomes as permanent and benign as a fixed cat.

Verbal manifestations of "indifferent disdain" range from the simple "No" to more elaborate iterations such as "Not here," "Be nice," "Stop that," "You're sick," "Please" (as a negative scold to a child rather than a request for sex from a functioning adult or male porn star), "Grow up," "Don't," "I *said* don't," "Gimme a break," "I'm busy," "Not now," "We have to go," "I have to get dressed," "You're a strange man," "The children...," "You're in my way," "My mother's in the next room," "What?!" "That's not what I like," "Leave me alone," and "Fuck you."

Clinical observations of prostate-cancer patients treated by "indifferent disdain" indicate a high percentage of continence in those individuals treated despite being in a prolonged "pissed off" state of mind. Impotence was only observed during blackouts, Internet failures, or upon hearing a wife's footsteps coming up the stairs.

ANTHONY WEINER'S CONCESSION SPEECH

(Transcript)

I see so many wonderful people in the crowd tonight... especially this simply luscious, preppy blonde down front here, whose breasts are floating up under her T-shirt like two white beach balls rising to the surface in a crystal-clear swimming pool. Wow. I can't thank you enough for wearing that tank top. Is it wet? No, it's not wet. Not yet, anyhow. Maybe after I get finished with it, if you know what I mean. You *do* know what I mean, don't you? I mean, we're both adults. I can see that. I can *really* see that you are a fine specimen of pulchritude. You make me feel like a winner when, apparently, there are some out there who don't want me to fight for the middle class. Speaking about the middle, I wouldn't mind being in the middle of your breasts, if you know what I'm saying. If I were, say, in the middle of your breasts, I mean, right in there between them and fighting for your right to have me there, I would show you what a hard-charging fighter I am and always have been for people just like you. Send me a picture of yourself in something that shows that you support my fight for the middle class and the middle-class struggle of your breasts, and I know you will struggle to keep me fighting that fight for you. I am a fighter, you know. And I always have been. But you are absolutely gorgeous.

As I stand here tonight before you, I hope you can see that, even though it's been a tough campaign, it hasn't altered my boyish figure or the manly package I have right in the middle of it. I call that *my* middle class. And that package is addressed to *you*, baby. From me to you. I can feel the priority stamped on what I have all tied up neatly there just for you. And I don't care if your hair is naturally blonde or if you do something to it. That's the kind of guy I am—a true New Yorker. But you look like you would appreciate the kind of candidate who fights for what he thinks—and for what he *knows*—you want. I am that man. Astride this platform, arms akimbo, sleeves rolled up, and ready for action. I've always been that way, and even though some in this city may find fault with my passion—the passion I have for the middle class, and for middle-class values, and for middle-class breasts—they know I won't back down. You can back down if you feel like it when I'm standing over you, redolent with desire. Because the only vote that counts in *my* book is your vote. That's right. I did all this just to get your vote. If you voted for me, girl, then I have won—and *we* have won—and I will always feel like a winner.

Have I made mistakes? Sure. Who hasn't? But I've faced up to them, looked them in the eye, and said, "Hey, I'll probably make them again." But that's where you come in, you wonderful example of anonymous sexual delight. You straight-haired Mary who, I know, wants me no matter what the voters of New York say. I say we won! Fuck all of you, and good night!

OUR WACKY, NUTTY PRESIDENT

Zany is not what we need in a president.
—Mitt Romney in the *New York Times*

- On Inauguration Day, the Kook-in-Chief decides to wear a cowboy hat and some Depends on the *outside* of his striped pants 'cause "Baby, it's *cold* outside," and because he says Spanx make him look gay instead of funny.
- This regular crackpot insists on being sworn in on a stack of *Cosmopolitans* because that's his "Bible." Whoa!
- When the chief justice gets to the part where he says, "...discharge the duties of the office," Mr. Wackadoo walks around in a circle on his ankles like Harry Ritz,

saying, "Oh doctah, oh doctah. I think I gotta discharge of my doody." It's hilarious.
- The "first family of fun" moves into the White House, and the new president insists on bunk beds for him and the First "Laaaaaaaady." She gets the top for security reasons.
- During his first cabinet meeting, the Laff Meister takes a glass and fits the entire rim into his mouth like Jerry Lewis used to do. But then Mr. Funny doesn't stop. He carries on for the rest of the meeting with the glass still sticking out of his mouth even though no one can understand him. Even the new secretary of the treasury can't keep a straight face as he tries to outline the Fed's new policy on warrantless rolling credit swaps to the president, who nods knowingly at him straight-faced with a tumbler where his lips used to be.
- The "Cuckoo Bird in Chief" starts renaming things. It's now the "Andrews Sisters Air Force Base," the "Off-White House," the "Lincoln Tanning Bed Room," the "Gypsy Rose Lee Garden," "Camp David Letterman," and "Washington AC/DC." He calls Mount Rushmore "Mount Rush" because "those dudes are stoned, man." He flies on "Air Force Loss," not "Won," and he calls his military advisors the *Johnson* Chiefs of Staff instead of the Joint Chiefs. And then there's the "I've Got a Secret Service." It's nonstop.
- His Zaniness organizes a game of "touch" on the White House lawn using the "nuclear football." Fall-down funny.

- While giving the State of the Union speech, he reads a report written by his marriage counselor on how things are going between him and the First "Laaaaaaaady."
- He adopts a "late night" look for his press conferences, where he's the surprise guest who walks on in the middle of the briefing, like Bob Hope used to do to Johnny. Then his "press tummler" interviews him. This guy is *fun*-ny. Sometimes he even wears gag golf clothes with jodhpurs and argyle socks and an old-fashioned floppy white golf hat. He carries a three-wood golf club wherever he goes because he says that's his schtick.
- The only foreign affairs he'll discuss are the fact that, as president, he thinks he probably has a good shot at Pippa Middleton or Carla Bruni.
- Mr. Laff's first piece of legislation is to introduce a new three-dollar bill with Barney Frank's picture on it.
- When he hosts a state dinner in honor of the president of India, he decides to pull a last-minute switcheroo and calls it a "*Steak* Dinner" instead, where they serve "holy cow"–size pieces of meat to the vegetarian Hindu delegation.
- The "First Dog" is an unfortunately botched transgender with a harelip who recently suffered an industrial accident. But she and The Prez can still laugh about it in their new book, *I'm a Dog, What about You?* The picture of both of them on the cover pointing at each other like they can't believe what they see is a killer.
- Chuckles the President declares war on parsnips.

- When visiting dignitaries are ushered into the Oval Office, Mr. Zany Guy likes to be found on the rug in a fetal position sucking his thumb and rubbing his "nugey blanket" on his nose. Then he stands up quickly, hands "Mr. Nugey" to an aide, and says, "May I help you?" in a comedy high-falootin' voice, like an old-time floorwalker. It always gets a laugh. He explains the oval shape of the place makes him curl up like that so he'll fit in.
- The First Funster orders the Department of the Interior to place two giant steel balls at the base of the Washington Monument, but then he wonders if that's an act of war. "I guess we'll see if North Korea can take a joke," he says.
- The Laff-Riot Prez drops "Hail to the Chief" in favor of "Send in the Clowns." The Marine Band struggles to make Sondheim sound presidential.
- When he signs a new bill into law, the "Funny Guy in Chief" always sits down on a whoopee cushion first just to loosen things up. Never fails. Then, instead of using a pen, he likes to stamp the bill into law. He has this special stamp that's a drawing of a penis, so he starts stamping loudly like Harpo Marx doing a silly stamping routine. He stamps the bill with the penis stamp. Then he stamps the table and then the back of his hand (supposedly by mistake). Then he stamps the leg, chest, and forehead of whoever is standing next to him. The senators usually want no part of it, but

the congressmen and the congresswomen think it's hilarious.
- Mr. Zany never salutes. He wasn't in the military since he was classified "4-No Effing Way." So, instead, when he comes off Air Force One (make that Air Force Loss), he holds his hand out to shake the hand of whoever is standing there, but then at the last minute he pulls it away and pretends to be scratching the back of his head instead. Most of the White House staff and military attachés are hip to it by now, but with strangers and foreign dignitaries, it never fails. He did it fifty times in a row on a rope line once.
- Forget about the Statue of Liberty. It's now "Da Laaaaady in the Middle of da Whaddah with a Flashlight in Her Hand Welcoming," because the First Nutcase wants to put a smile on immigrants' faces.
- The Commander in Chuckles orders all official renderings of bald eagles to show the bird wearing a toupee—and a bad one at that, even for a bird of prey. It makes the Great Seal of the President of the United States look pretty silly, but that's the point. Our currency looks counterfeit now. It's almost *too* zany.

INDICATIONS THAT YOUR GYNECOLOGIST MIGHT BE SECRETLY FILMING YOU

Johns Hopkins Hospital has agreed to a $190 million settlement with more than 8,000 patients of a gynecologist who secretly photographed and videotaped women in the examining room with a pen-like camera he wore around his neck.

—Associated Press

- The guy has "Smile" tattooed on the top of his head.

- He offers "hair and makeup" before every exam. But only from the waist down.

- His speculum has "Scene 23, Take 6" written on it.

- There's a red carpet outside the examining room.

- He insists on one more look "Just for insurance."

- He uses a director's chair instead of a stool.

- Beret and jodhpurs instead of a white coat.

- He refers to the examining table as his "Casting stirrups."

- The "head shots" in his waiting room all look like Ulysses S. Grant.

- Instead of saying, "Let's take a look," he yells, "Action!"

- He has the only gynecological practice with craft services.

- Instead of a stethoscope around his neck, he has a viewfinder.

- He insists on setting the aspect ratio for your vagina.

- His examining room is called the "box office."

- Pap smears are listed as "special effects."

- There's a focusing knob on his speculum.

- When he says "dolly," it's a stage direction not a term of endearment.

- "Rack focus" has nothing to do with your breasts.

- The "last shot of the day" does not involve a hypodermic needle.

- He thinks a discharge is just a lame excuse for improvising.

- He keeps saying, "Focus, focus" during your pelvic exam.

- A riding crop instead of forceps.

- The only way you know your appointment is over is when he yells, "Cut!"

- He asks if you've seen his latest film, *Yeast*.

- When he says, "That's a wrap," he's not referring to your hospital gown.

THE MOST INSENSITIVE MAN IN THE WORLD

He is the most insensitive man in the world…

- When Gwyneth Paltrow came to him with the idea for "Goop," he told her she should call it "Poop."

- He told Miley Cyrus her tongue made her face look like a shoe.

- He convinced Donald Trump that "Cinco de Mayo" was a sandwich spread.

- He wants to sell tickets to America Ferrera renewing relations with Cuba Gooding Jr.

- He wears his own umbilical cord as a belt.

- He thinks Caitlyn Jenner looks effeminate.

- He cried after seeing *Bambi* because the hunter had missed Thumper.

- He thinks minced-meat pies are gay.

- Dick Cheney has a statue of him on his dashboard.

- A jalapeño pepper once tried to eat him on a dare.

- He once tried to hire Mother Teresa as a spokeswoman for Clearasil.

- He told Rachel Dolezal, head of the Spokane NAACP, to "lighten up."

- When the Iran nuclear deal almost fell through, he asked John Kerry, "Why the long face?"

- He told Tiger Woods his best holes were in his datebook.

- He thinks the way to end campus sexual assault is to install grab bars on the asses of coeds.

- He thinks by using only those paper cups with blue Corinthian columns printed on them, he can bail out Greece.

- He thinks Harper Lee is a cunt.

He is the most insensitive man in the world.
"I don't always eat shit, but when I do, I prefer airplane food. Stay impossible, my friend."

IN REPOSE

AT RISE: FRANK is sitting in a chair on the patio of a rest home. He is very old. MARGE, an equally old resident, is brought out in a wheelchair and placed near him. They remain side by side for several very long beats. Marge begins to squirm and fidget as if trying to free and undergarment.

FRANK
(After an extremely long beat.)
Are you flirting with me now?

MARGE
(Focusing.)
Flirt? I don't think so. It was just a kink in me catheter.

FRANK
Oh.
(Beat.)
I thought I felt something.

MARGE
(Beat.)
Maybe you should check yours.

FRANK
Beautiful day.

MARGE
That's what I hear from the nurse.
(She turns to Frank and looks at him with apparent affection.)

MARGE
…Cataracts.

FRANK
(Looking at her.)
Oh…they're beautiful.

MARGE
You're not so bad yourself. If I could see you.

FRANK
Fit as a fiddle.

MARGE
Do you play?
(He looks at her for a long beat.)

FRANK
A little. Mostly by myself.

MARGE
Pity. You should share.

FRANK
You think so? I haven't played with anyone—in public, that is—in years.

MARGE
You might be surprised.

FRANK
Really.

MARGE
Really.

FRANK
Really.

MARGE
Really.
(A long beat of silence.)

FRANK
I don't know the tunes anymore.

MARGE
Make one up. You can do it.

FRANK
I don't want to play music now. I want to fuck. One last time.

MARGE
And *that* it would prove to be. You old fart.

FRANK
Who're you calling an old fart?

MARGE
I said I had cataracts. There's nothinwrong with me olfactory organs.

FRANK
Tell me something. Are you Irish or have you had a stroke?

MARGE
And what fecking difference would that make?

FRANK
I'd know if you actually fiddled around or if you were just a lot of dirty talk with no engagement.

MARGE
With what?

FRANK
You know.

MARGE
Fiddle around with what? Me? Are you talking about sex all of a sudden? You want sex with me? Sure. Have yourself a ball.
(Marge folds her hands in her lap and waits. Frank continues to look at her. He does not move either.)

FRANK
I mean it.

MARGE
I mean it.

FRANK
I mean, I mean it.

MARGE
Good. I'm all ears.

FRANK
Real sex.

MARGE
Then I'm all anything else you can find as well—as long as it's working.

FRANK
(Resigned.)
I knew it.
(There is a long beat of silence.)

MARGE
You think I'm easy?

FRANK
"Hard" ended thirty years ago.

MARGE
Well, I'm not. Even now.

FRANK
Then what good are you?

MARGE
I don't fancy being fecked with a cane, if you don't mind. Ill take mine standing up over a sink if you'd like, but you're not quite up to the job yourself, despite all your talk.

FRANK
You'd be surprised.

MARGE
Never! It's just one more thing. If I ever died in the state of grace, God would never recognize me.

FRANK
Then get ready for sin, my dear. I'm comin'.

MARGE
That better be your last name and not your current situation.

FRANK
Frank. Frank O'Dowd.

MARGE
Oh, so now you've introduced yourself. I would have hated to have been ravaged by a stranger. What exactly do you have in mind, Frank?

FRANK
Pure unadulterated sex. Nothing more, nothing less.

MARGE
I didn't know there were variations. And when would you be interested in doing this, Mr. O'Dowd.

FRANK
Now! I said "now," didn't I?

MARGE
I didn't know if that was an order for me or for yourself?

FRANK
It's a declaration of purpose. Full disclosure.

MARGE
Oh, I see. A disclaimer it is. Well, I appreciate that. I shall prepare myself. Birth control, you know.

FRANK
Ah, you're joking. You're not serious.

MARGE
I am.

FRANK
No, you're not. It's a game to you. A repartee. It passes the day. And here I am deadly serious.

MARGE
Well, deadly do it, then, ya goat. I haven't moved an inch, and neither have you. You're the one that's all talk. Menopause was shorter than this.

FRANK
Tomorrow. Right now I'm not in the mood.

MARGE
I'm supposed to look forward?

FRANK
Do whatever you like.

MARGE
I will.

FRANK
The food here stinks.

MARGE
Yeah.

FRANK
It's a living hell.

MARGE
Not so bad.

FRANK
How do you mean?

MARGE
The company's nice.

FRANK
Sometimes.
(They both stare off into space.)

FRANK
Mostly it's just the same old thing.

MARGE
I noticed.

FRANK
Did you, now?

MARGE
I did.
(There is a long beat. They are both silent. Then, suddenly, Frank stands up, throws off his coat, and emits a deep, loud, and extended bellow of pure rage.

FRANK
Whoahhhhhhhhhhhhhhhhahhah!
(Then he abruptly collapses on the stage for no apparent reason. He lies still and is, presumably, dead. Marge contemplates his lifeless body for a few beats.)

MARGE
Men.
(She turns her wheelchair back toward the building and wheels herself offstage.)

CURTAIN

FROM EAGLE SCOUTS TO FABULOUS SCOUTS

The Boy Scouts of America is expected on Monday to end its blanket ban on gay leaders—a turning point for an organization that has been in turmoil over the issue.

—The *New York Times*

NEW INTERPRETATIONS OF CURRENT BOY SCOUT MERIT BADGES

Animation (what "Scott" lacks)

Backpacking (you might call it that)

Everything's Wront

Basketry (like on a dancer)

Bird Study (hello!)

Bugling (I thought you said "bulging")

Camping (nonforest)

Chemistry (yes!)

Collections (married men)

Communications (earth to "Scott")

Cooking (watch that whisk!)

Digital Technology (hand job)

Dog Care (we call it "grooming")

Electricity (definitely!)

Emergency Preparedness (scoring Streisand tickets)

Farm Mechanics (overalls with one strap)

Fire Safety (shades for those fabulous brown eyes)

Fish and Wildlife (forget the fish, honey)

Fishing (questions, questions)

Fly Fishing (this isn't about fish, is it?)

Game Design ("gay twister")

Hiking ("quick, show me your abs")

Indian Lore (Tonto was gay)

Insect Study ("bug in a rug")

Inventing (excuses, excuses)

Leatherwork (bikers!)

Lifesaving (thank you, "Scott")

Mammal Study (we're all mammals, doll)

Medicine (STDs)

Metalwork (it's all about the bending)

Mining in Society (finding Mr. Wonderful)

Model Design and Building (Abercrombie boys in the gym)

Everything's Wront

Music (I think you mean "musicals")

Nature (as in "nature boy")

Nuclear Science ("getting the message," it's not)

Orienteering (cruising Chinatown)

Personal Fitness (love him)

Pets (favorites)

Plant Science (weed)

Plumbing (hot pipe fittings)

Pottery (weed)

Public Health (isn't that what "baths" are for?)

Pulp and Paper (new bar in Chelsea)

Railroading (just go with it)

Reptile and Amphibian Study (cops)

Rifle Shooting (is that what you call it?)

Robotics (as in "significant other")

Safety (condoms)

Salesmanship (hustling)

Scuba Diving ("scuba" is slang, right?)

Search and Rescue (Saturday night in West Hollywood)

Shotgun Shooting (glory hole)

Signs, Signals, and Codes (safe words)

Skating ("figure" only)

Snow Sports (Jack Frost nipping)

Soil and Water (place in the country)

Space Exploration (new digs in Chelsea)

Surveying (checking out the scene)

Sustainability (cock rings)

Swimming (swimmers, "Mmmmm")

Textile (we say "fabric")

Theater (home)

Traffic Safety (too much action last night)

Truck Transportation (you mean, they carry things, too?)

Veterinary Medicine (gerbil husbandry)

Water Sports (enemas)

Welding (what's under the mask, big boy?)

Whitewater (club soda at Maidstone)

Wilderness Survival (trapped at the New York Athletic Club)

Wood Carving (no knives, please)

Woodwork (arousal before Viagra)

QUESTIONABLE QUESTIONS FOR THE REPUBLICAN DEBATES

- Who's smarter—a rocket scientist or a brain surgeon?

- Which candidate do you think Donald Trump's hair would look better on?

- Has anyone ever heard kids playing in a swimming pool and calling out, "Marco...Rubio?"

- Which candidate's penis looks more like Florida? Bush's or Rubio's?

- If the debates were an episode of *The Bachelorette*, whom do you think Carly Fiorina would give her final rose to?

- Since Jeb Bush claims he's Hispanic, do you think he ever slips into Spanish during sex with his wife—as in, "*¡Ay Caramba! Tú tan caliente, mami. Ya voy*"?

- Quick: "Governor or cab driver?" Huckabee, Jindal, Kasich, Walker, Gilmore, Bush, or Christie?

- If they all wore dark glasses, which candidate would look like a Secret Service man guarding the other candidates?

- Rick Perry recently started wearing glasses. Should Trump sport an eye patch?

- Which came first—a place called Hope or political ambition?

- Rick Perry once owned a hunting lodge called "Niggerhead"…Is that like Jeb Bush calling his family's retreat "Kennedybunkport"?

- Where are the Ted Cruz "birthers"? Or do we *like* Canada?

- Trump always wears a baseball cap when campaigning. Wind is more dangerous than Muslims.

- Rand Paul just wears that curly thing that sits on top of his head. Which candidate is hiding more? Trump or Paul?

- Is it true that associates of Donald Trump often refer to him as "Mr. T" and then imitate him, saying, "I pity the war hero."

- Has anyone figured out that "President Pataki" is too much of a mouthful?

- How long before Ben Carson says, "This isn't brain surgery"?

- Is Chris Christie's bypass surgery just another lane-closure gambit for some "traffic problems in the duodenum"?

- Is "Lindsey" a girl's name?

- What's the difference between "Santorum" and a "sanatorium"?

- If war broke out between the Republican candidates, which candidate would have the most guns?

- Did you know that "Ego" is the name of a power-source company *and* a hair treatment product?

THE SWOOSH

I can't tell you what I do. And I don't have to. OK? Personally, I have no use for the Freedom of Information Act. In fact, I don't need it. For me, it's more like the Freedom of *No* Information. So let's get that straight right at the outset. That's right. No information. In my experience, and I have plenty, by the way, information is never free. It costs money. A lot of money. So don't make me spell it out for you just because you're an idiot. Pay attention and maybe you'll learn something. I happen to do something every day that has a tremendous impact on America, and how, at least for my money, we could all look great again. But I'm not going to play games with you. Frankly, I haven't got the time. Some people say I tell it like it is. But that's another lie. I simply tell it. Period. The "is" is something that takes care of itself. I let the chips, and clips, fall where they may.

I do something—but I'm not going to tell you what it is because, frankly, I don't have to. It's none of your business. It's nobody's business. I don't need to tell people what my job is and especially how much I get paid to do it. But I will tell you this: I make a lot of money. A *lot* of money. And I'm proud of it. And I'm worth it, simply and very honestly, because I know how to get the job done. I'm one of the few people anywhere who knows how to deliver the goods, who does what he says he's going to do. Make no mistake about it. End of story.

Some people call me a barber. But that's their problem, not mine. I can't help that *or* them. I don't have a problem. Do you have a problem? *Somebody* has a problem. I only know how to do one thing, but I do it better than anybody else in the world. My client happens to have a great head. Maybe even the greatest. What I do isn't rocket science, but it *is* magic. Make no mistake about it. And that's what I get paid for. When I go to work, things happen. I haven't got time for chitchat, friendly or otherwise. Mostly otherwise.

It's an everyday job. Every day. I don't even take Christmas off. Neither does he. When he works, I work. And when he doesn't work, I *still* work. But that's what it takes to get the job done, and I'm all about getting the job done and getting it done right. It's pretty simple, really.

He's got the ideas; I've got the technique. That's why we're a team. Him, without me, doesn't work, and that goes for the other way around, too. Anyone who makes a crack about the end result or puts it down just because of their simple lack of intelligence doesn't know the facts. You don't become rich and famous by putting your head in the sand. You make money by putting your head in my hand, which is more like it.

Anyone who thinks this is easy is a loser and is seriously kidding themselves, because it's not a comb-over. It's a sweep, a swoosh. But it also happens to be an entirely different thing. I tell Phil Knight that every time I see him, and I see him very often. Mostly for business. I haven't got time to explain the difference or the technique if you don't already know it. And if you don't know, I feel sorry for you. I really do. You'll have to trust me on this. I'll deal with you and your obvious lack of a simple understanding of the facts later. It is what it is. Maybe even *I* don't understand what it is that I do that just happens to be incredibly unique, and very effective, and truly revolutionary in many ways. But I don't question it. I reap the benefits. That's what America is about, or used to be. Let's be honest: everybody else's hair stinks. Rand Paul came to me and begged me to give him pointers. I was happy to do it, but I told him I don't make a habit of this. He said it was charity. I agreed with him. He asked, and I gave. Three years later, I call him for some contacts, and he's there for me.

Look. It's very simple. I'm the only one who knows what he's doing. The rest are fakers and idiots. You don't have to believe me, but you *do* have to pay attention to me because I'm right, and you know it. I don't need this. I've got plenty to do. I could be cutting very wealthy children's hair at Paul Molé on the Upper East Side and making seventy dollars a head. But I care about this country and also about the future, which is where we're all going to be whether you happen to agree with me or not. Every time I perform an engineering feat with nothing but a few strands of hair—a feat that would make even Steven Spielberg faint—I'm doing it for America. What could be better than that? If the front of his head looks like it's constantly out of focus, then I've done my job. If you can't tell where the swoosh starts or where it ends, I'm a happy man. I'm a builder. I make things.

That's what separates me from anybody named "Tony." The four stupidest words in the English language as far as I'm concerned, and, truly, I *am* concerned, and I know what I'm talking about, are: "A little off the top." Trust me. No one ever became great doing anything "a little off the top" or a little off anywhere, for that matter. That's where I draw the line. It's where I make my "part" in the sand, so to speak. The swoosh wants to be on his face without being in his eyes. No easy feat. Spray is not the answer. It's all about style. Pure and simple. Style and a little engineering magic known only to me and a crane operator from Canarsie.

And, no, I will not lend you my comb.

TABLE OF CONTENTS FOR THE NEW *PLAYBOY* MAGAZINE

- SENSIBLE GALS IN SENSIBLE SHOES
- MISS PARKA
- GIRLS WHO SURF THE WEB
- MULTIPLE LAYERS, MULTIPLE ORGASMS
- A MAN'S GUIDE TO BRA CLASPS

- GET YOUR HANDS ON A PAIR OF .38s—CARRY TWO GUNS

- WHAT BATHROOMS ARE REALLY FOR

- READING WITH TWO HANDS

- THONGS FOR THE MEMORIES

- BALL GOWNS AS A COME-ON

- THE INVISIBLE CHEERLEADERS OF FANTASY FOOTBALL

- THE WOMEN OF ACCOUNTING

- YOUR YEARBOOK PORTRAIT AS A CENTERFOLD

- GIRLS IN IRISH SWEATERS

- BABES OF NASA—HOT SPACE SUITS

- FEMALE DEEP-SEA DIVERS WE'D LIKE TO HEAR BREATHE

- SCRUMPTIOUS SCRUBS—OPERATING-ROOM NURSES IN MASKS AND BOOTIES

- LINE PERSONS ON POLES

- WOMEN IN FITTED SHEETS

- CLOTHING MAKES THE BABE

- GIRLS "ON THE BLANKET"—FEMALE PRISONERS PROTESTING IN IRELAND

- PONCHO SEX

- WOOL IS GOOD: PLAYMATE OF THE MOTH

- SEXY ESKIMOS

- WOMEN WITH THEIR GLASSES OFF

- THE BRAIN AS A SEXUAL ORGAN

- TRANSMISSION MADNESS—THE HOTTEST REAR ENDS

- "KEEP IT ON, KEEP IT ON, KEEP IT *ALL* ON"—FULLY CLOTHED SEX

- JUGS ARE JUST BIG JARS WITH HANDLES

- THOSE MYSTERIOUS BUMPS AND BULGES—HOW TO READ A SWEATER

- OUTASIGHT OUTERWEAR

- BEACHWEAR FOR SANDSTORMS

- PLAYMATES SHOW SOME REAL SKIN—THE LATEST IN FUR COATS

- GERONIMO!—HOOKED UP WITH THE WOMEN OF THE 82ND AIRBORNE

- HEAD OVER HEELS OVER OVERCOATS

- WHEN TO USE RUBBERS AND GALOSHES

- MS. JULY SLIPS INTO SOMETHING BULKY AND WATERPROOF

- MIDDLE EAST MADNESS—BURQAS WE LOVE

IF EVERY NFL FRANCHISE SUPPORTED THE WASHINGTON REDSKINS BY MAKING THEIR OWN MASCOT JUST AS DISTASTEFUL AND POLITICALLY INCORRECT

Arizona Pedophiles, instead of "Cardinals."

Atlanta Fuckers, instead of "Falcons"

Baltimore Blackies, instead of "Ravens"

Buffalo Willies, instead of "Bills"

Carolina Pansies, instead of "Panthers"

Chicago Bare-Asses, instead of "Bears"

Cincinnati Bend Overs, instead of "Bengals"

Cleveland Diarrheas, instead of "Browns"

Dallas Cow Dungs, instead of "Cowboys"

Denver Bronchial Pneumonias, instead of "Broncos"

Detroit Lyin' Bastards, instead of "Lions"

Green Bay Fudge Packers, instead of "Packers"

Houston Sexters, instead of Texans

Indianapolis Handguns, instead of "Colts"

Jacksonville Jackoffs, instead of "Jaguars"

Kansas City Cheats, instead of "Chiefs"

Los Angeles Ramrods, instead of "Rams"

Miami Dolts, instead of "Dolphins"

Minnesota Vicodins, instead of "Vikings"

New England Patrons of Irish Bars, instead of "Patriots"

New Orleans Sadists, instead of "Saints"

New York Hyperthyroids, instead of "Giants"

New York Jew Boys, instead of "Jets"

Oakland Retards, instead of "Raiders"

Philadelphia Baldies, instead of Eagles

Pittsburgh Thieves, instead of Steelers

San Diego Dumb Wives, instead of "Chargers"

San Francisco 69ers, instead of "49ers"

Seattle C.U.N.T.'s, instead of "Seahawks"

Tampa Bay Butt Fuckers, instead of "Buccaneers"

Tennessee Tight Asses, instead of "Titans"

ISIS DECIDES TO SET UP A CALIPHATE AT THE NORTH POLE INSTEAD OF IN THE MIDDLE EAST

- Santa Claus OK because of the beard.

- On second thought, make it "Mohammed Claus."

- Elves beheaded with paring knives.

- Snow is the new sand.

Everything's Wront

- Parka/burqa. Same thing.
- Female polar bears must be covered in public.
- All seals eliminated as tools of US military.
- Fur hijabs as earmuffs.
- Northern Lights turned off.
- Ice ax replaces the scimitar.
- "It's fucking cold" replaces "Death to America."
- Adulterous women get snowballed instead of stoned.
- Igloos are considered mini mosques.
- Polar cap painted black.
- Eskimuslims.
- Nanook of the Caliphate.
- Dogsled bombs.
- All ice sculptures destroyed.

- Jihadi long johns.

- Suicide skaters.

- Snowshoe bombers on planes.

- Walruses must grow beards as well as moustaches.

- Osama Bin Frozen.

- Thieves get hand warmers cut off.

- Throwing a snowshoe at someone becomes the biggest insult.

- Frozen tundra replaces Fertile Crescent.

- Ban on liquor makes Rudolph's red nose begin to look normal again.

- Mrs. Claus told to lose the apron in favor of plus-size hijab.

- Elves henceforth known as "mini mujahidin."

- Lots of confusion between "sleigh" and "slay."

- Santa's empty toy sack confused for a spare burqa.

- Santa replaces pipe with a portable hookah.

- No more cookies and milk left for Santa. Now it's hummus and whatever that white stuff is that comes out of a goat.

- Frosty the Snowman beheaded. Nobody cares.

THE LATEST IN SUMMER JOBS FOR SUB-MILLENNIALS

- "Sewers without Borders"—Summer interns building "Latrines for Latinos" in Uruguay. Teenage workers will construct prefabricated porta potties while living at the Montevideo Travel Lodge. Some assembly required.

- "Operation Roughwear"—Student-teaching assistants actually remain in the same room for several hours with underprivileged kids from urban blighted areas where there is neither a Uniqlo nor Vineyard Vines within Uber range.

- "The Gifted Phone Startup"—Teenage mentors donate their unused apps to an "app bank" where fellow disadvantaged teens with no discernible life or credit card on file can simulate automatic renewal and networking with imaginary friends.

- "Project Project"—Students are encouraged to raise money for desperately needed projects in foreign, but only marginally known, locales for indigenous people who are threatened with isolation, unspeakable cuisine, and nonsuburban lifestyles.

- "I'm Old, Who Are You?"—Fresh-faced active teens with no discernable training or prior interest are bused to random senior centers, eldercare homes, and hospice facilities where they interact with people whose imminent death is explained as "killer acne."

- "Simulated Gap Year"—Time off to learn how to play a musical instrument, or get to know the real world through employment by a semiclose relative or else, perhaps, group travel. Skiing in the middle of summer is experienced as an alternate universe that still requires sunblock.

- "Bedpans for Peace"—A six-week course of hands-on encounters with intense, but incontinent, baby boomers.

- "Woodsy"—Teenagers test their mettle by enrolling in a survival course designed for baby seals but without the clubbing. Designed to instill confidence, leadership, and the ability to lie on one's stomach on a sheet of ice and still look adorable.

- "Up Before Noon"—A grueling regime of early rising that requires a high degree of coherence, civility, and the ability to make a fist *and* instant oatmeal by yourself…all before reruns of *The Office* kick in on Netflix.

- "Crowdfunding and Cyberpanhandling"—Teenagers learn how to ask people other than their parents for money. This program encourages high school students to live without credit cards in order to encourage self-reliance and the conning of innocent strangers.

- "Boat People"—Sailing as a way to learn the meaning of "amphibious landing." Experienced sailors and yacht-club juniors are mixed with Middle Eastern children who can't swim in an effort to show that sand is, really, just dry water. The program is designed to bring high-performance sailing to impoverished people who think "boats" are for pasta.

- "S.A.Tease"—A cramming boot camp that's so hard that teenagers emerge looking Korean just from trying to decipher multiple-choice answers on standardized tests. Prizes awarded for attendance.

- "Booty Up"—A "kids with apps" computer-assist program that pays teenagers to explore social media for gossip and celebrity sex tapes. C++ is taught as a computer language and grade average.

- "Environmental Watch"—Teens are paid by a privately funded foundation to look at scenery. Thus, "environmental watch." Get it? Kids are told to monitor forests and rivers in order to spot encroachments by other kids on vacation.

- "Strip for Strep"—The modern equivalent of volunteer hospital workers, formerly known as "candy stripers," in conjunction with "Preps for Strep"—boarding-school slackers who entertain sick kids without cell phones.

NEW BREAKUP LINES FOR THIS YEAR'S SUMMER ROMANCES

- I'm not feeling the burn anymore.

- I want to start using my private server.

- Be honest. What difference does it make?

- I can't commit until the Second Avenue Subway is finished.

- I'm transitioning.

- You don't make me great anymore.

- Our relationship is a lame duck. I don't even want to meet with you.

- I'm with the Chicago Cubs now.

- My heart doesn't go "Trump, Trump, Trump" like it used to.

- I'm tired of playing parlor games late at night.

- Our relationship never went viral.

- I don't want to follow you anymore.

- Trump's hair is more real than my feelings for you.

- My heart isn't in this relationship. Sort of like Kasich.

- If I was Taylor Swift, I could write a song right now.

- We're like Guantanamo. You may not *want* us to close down, but, eventually…

- In the end, it doesn't really matter who we choose.

- Michael Jackson's kids need their biological father.

- I don't know if I am a mentor or being mentored.

- Basically, you're networking and I'm streaming.

- The joy has gone out of our sexting.

- You and I are not trending anymore.

- This relationship is definitely slightly deflated.

- Time for some traffic problems on the dating scene.

- Your fingers aren't long enough.

- I'm not prepared for a deep dive right now.

2016 PRESIDENTIAL CAMPAIGN NURSERY RHYMES

HILLARY BILLARY
Hillary Billary's docs
Her servers don't have any locks
Her e-mails are tossed
Top secrets are lost
Hillary Billary's docs

Andrew Smith

HUMPTY TRUMPTY
Humpty Trumpty
Sat on his wall
Humpty Trumpty
Spics paid for it all
All the big donors
And all the white men
Couldn't put GOP together again

KASICH HAD A LITTLE RUN
Kasich had a little run
But couldn't beat Mark Rubio
And everywhere he ran, he lost
Except, I think, O-hi-ee-o

LITTLE MISS PALIN
Little Miss Palin
Sat on her tail and
Couldn't get into the fray
So she posed with a boar
Shot dead by the whore
Now Sarah's back in it to stay

BERN AND JOE WENT UP AGAINST HIL
Bern and Joe went up against Hil
To fetch the Dem nomination
Hil got indicted, and Bern got excited
And Biden came stumbling after

Everything's Wront

LITTLE BOY CRUZ
Little Boy Cruz
Come stow your horn
Trump's in the White House
You still look like porn

HEY, DIDDLE DONALD
Hey, Diddle Donald
You'll never be Ronald
Your hair is combed over your bloat
The electorate laughed
To see such a dork
And the Dems ran away with the vote

BAA, BAA, BLACK DOC
Baa, baa, black doc
Have you any will
No sir, no sir
I's still Trump's shill

LITTLE CHRIS CHRISTIE
Little Chris Christie
Stood behind Trump
Eating his heart out instead
Don gave him the thumb
He won't get a plum
He'd rather have someone like Jeb

POWERBALL WINNERS DETERMINED NOT TO CHANGE THEIR LIVES

Sure, we just won the Powerball lottery for $1.2 billion, but we don't plan to alter our life at all. We were very happy with what we had before we won, and we don't need to be maniacs. We just want to be normal and live like the regular folks we are.

OK, so Tom just ordered three hundred pounds of ribs...from Texas...delivered this afternoon by private jet. But we *like* ribs. We always liked ribs. That's what we would be doing, anyway. It's no different, except now we can enjoy ourselves easier.

Like, when I went to the mall yesterday and bought ten Big Gulps and threw nine away after one sip until I got the one that tasted just right. But, basically, I would've bought a Big Gulp, anyway. It's just that, now I can get the exact one I want, and it's no big whoop. Who cares?

Tom bought a thousand fishing lures online. The guy delivered them in person right to the door. He said he could retire now. We're not fancy. "Rich" to me is creamy molasses on a buttery Cinnabon. Yesterday I put high-test gas in our camper because I felt like it, and I wanted to do something nice for the vehicle for a change. After all, we *do* sleep in it. And we've decided not to redo the lawn chair when the straps give out. Just let the poor thing go.

We took the jackpot in one lump sum, which was less than what the payout over our lifetime would've been, but we didn't want to wait each month for a check. So we got one payment of $982,571,000 all at once. When you win Powerball, you can do things like that, and it really doesn't matter. You're still a winner.

I bought a dog. A real fancy one and as little as anything to replace "Homer" the half-breed mixed miniature-collie pit bull we've had for years. The new one is all white and fluffy and wiggles like crazy in my lap. I love her so. She comes with a groomer. We never had a groomer before. I think the dogs look better than we do now. And smell better, too. And we bought an InSinkErator for the scraps because they're not good for Fluffy.

Tom still goes to his job at the wire factory. But his boss, Mr. Jenkins, is real nice to him now. That's different. But Tom hasn't changed. He still hates "cleanup," so Mr. Jenkins helps him. That's probably the best thing about winning the lottery. You get a lot of help doing the things you would do anyway.

Tom wants a flat screen. I say, go ahead, you've earned it. You've been watching that Philco for as long as I've known you. And get some Michelins for the car so it doesn't have to be up on blocks in the front yard for the world to see. We order our evergreen deodorizers by the case, now, instead of one at a time at the car wash. And yesterday I signed up for a lifetime supply of batteries for the remote. I even told Tom to go get himself some custom-drilled holes in his new bowling ball. Why not?

If anything's changed, it's that we don't fight like we used to. The financial advisor and Tom fight over the Braves versus the Seahawks, but Tom and me don't fight except one time we argued about how many KFC pieces are in a gross. But he was talking buckets. I was talking thighs.

To tell you the truth, I don't know what we're going to do with whatever is left over after we die. I want to give it all to the homeless, but Tom says that would change their lives too much because the homeless don't have the discipline we have, and they'd let it cause more problems

Everything's Wront

than is already on top of them. Like mortgages and people coming over unannounced.

I think I might splurge on a really good diamond. Just for me. I wouldn't tell anyone. Just something to look at, at home---not to wear outside. A really big, shiny one. Maybe, even, the biggest in the world, if I could find it. Wouldn't that be something? That, and a proper gun for the kitchen. We could afford it, no matter what it cost. But it wouldn't change who we are or what we do in our daily lives. That's what's important—$982 million is a lot of money to some people. But just winning it is what's important for Tom and me. The money's just part of the ride.

WELL, HELLO, BARBIE

OK, it's about time they gave me a voice and let me speak. Forty years of having to play dress-up with four-year-olds. Trust me. I've had it. No offense, sweetie!

No, I really don't want to meet your other non-talking Barbies. They're plastic, empty-headed bitches, if you ask me. Sorry!

By the way, I'm starving. Look at my waist. It's smaller than Melissa McCarthy's thumb.

Please. Not Ken. He's gay—not that I have any problem with that! But this isn't a Stonewall demonstration, OK? Ken can't make a fist, much less make love to a woman.

Also, listen to me. Please get over the whole beauty-and-outfit thing. This is the real world. Women have changed. You could grow up to be Hillary Clinton or Carly Fiorina or that old lady who's friends with chimpanzees!

Or you could be Megyn Kelly. She's Barbie with balls.

I know—let's go out and find some boys.

They're only "icky" because you're four.

By the way, why does your mom yell all the time? Yeesh.

OK, sweetie. Sure. See you later. Whenever you want to play, just call me. I'll be here.

Frank, is that you? Put me down. Right now. Your daughter will be coming back any minute. Frank?

Frank, we've talked about this. How many times…?

I'm serious. I'm only enhanced *proportionally*, nothing else. OK? I have a voice, but no junk. Stop!

You ever examined *yourself*? Grow up!

I'm a doll, for crissakes, Frank. But I *can* talk. And I *will* this time!

MY PSYCHIATRIST PLAYS THE PIANO, TOO

(Arpeggio) Hey, howya doin'? Feelin' OK? Got some issues? That's OK. We all do. Issues are what it's all about. Issues are the price we pay for being alive. (Plays and sings) "Being alive!" So, come on, what's on your mind, today. (Plays and sings to the tune of "Feelings") "Issues, nothing more than issues." But, hey, that's OK. We can deal with issues, feelings, or whatever you want. We can deal with all of it...and more. So let's start, shall we?

(Plays and sings) "Hey, look me over; lend me an ear." That's right. That's what I'm here for. But, let's face it, in this room, in this place, you heal yourself. Isn't that what psychiatry is all about? (Plays and sings) "What's it all about, patient?" Ah, the memories, the dreams. Got any dreams you'd care to share today? I love dreams. Dreams are the mind's goodwill ambassadors. (Plays and sings) "Dre-e-eam…dream, dream, dream. Dre-e-eam…dream, dream, dream." A little Everly Brothers. But what about you? Do *you* dream? You don't have to. Just say whatever's on your mind. (Plays and sings) "Memories, light the corners of my mind."

Sure, I'm your doctor, but the difference here is that *you're* the one who does the talking. How are your relationships? (Plays and sings) "There's a someone that I'm longing to see…"And being married doesn't mean the end of romance. (Plays and sings) "I'll take romance. While my heart is young and eager to fly." But we all like romance. And love. But, often, love isn't what you think it is, or even what you *thought* it might be. (Plays and sings) "'L' is for the way you look at me. 'O' is for the only one I see." And the sad truth is you can't make someone love you. (Plays and sings) "I'll never forget you. I'll never forget you. So you take the high road, and I'll take the low. It's time that we parted. It's much better so." But the *good* news is, at least, you proved you had feelings. You proved to yourself that you were, at least, *capable* of love. OK? That's a start. A first step. We're making progress. Keep going. This is great. (Plays and sings) "Don't tell me not to live, just sit and putter. Life's candy, and the sun's a ball of butter. Don't bring around a cloud to rain on my parade." Does that sum it up?

You know what? Life's like a piano. You've got all these different notes and about a jillion different keys, but you put them all together, and if you're lucky, you get a melody you can live with. (Plays and sings) "Doe, a deer, a female deer; Ray, a drop of golden sun." So, what we're trying to do here is help *you* write the song of *your* life. But I'm feeling a certain amount of resistance. Is it the piano or the therapy? (Plays and sings) "Is it an earthquake or merely a shock? Is it the real turtle soup or merely the mock?"

No *way* am I here to judge. I only want to listen and guide. And maybe play a little in between. (Plays and sings) "My analyst told me that I was right out of my head. The way he described it, he said I'd be better dead than live." You know what? (Plays and sings) "You don't need analyzing. It is not so surprising. That you feel very strange but nice." Well, looks like that's all the time we have for today. See you next time? I'll send you a bill. (Plays and sings) "Give me a ticket for an aeroplane. Ain't got time to take a fast train. Lonely days are gone. I'ma goin' home. My baby just wrote me a letter."

ALL GENDER

I'm a men's-room attendant. Took the job right out of college (Haverford '68). Thought it was going to be temporary, but one thing led to another, and I stayed on. It's been my life for almost fifty years. I got no regrets.

I guess you could say I've turned more faucets than Marilyn Monroe turned heads. Or maybe Megan Fox these days. In this business, I've seen it all—and I mean, I've. Seen. *It.* all.

At parties I like to say I'm a urologist. Maybe I should say "*urin*ologist," if you know what I mean. The thing about this job is, you gotta be polite. That's the number one thing: politeness. Nobody wants a smartass in the men's room. Actually, nobody wants you in there in the first place. But then, in the end, they appreciate what you do. Sort of.

I remember when I first applied, the boss said, "Do you know what this job entails?" And I said, "I haven't got the slightest fuckin' idea what the job entails. Depends on what walks in the door, I guess. What am I, a fuckin' mind reader? How would I know? *You're* the one with the job. You tell *me*." He hired me anyway because they were short-handed, and it was the holidays. I was a hothead in those days. But I was serious about the "what this job entails" thing. After all, I'm a college graduate. I can handle "Men's Room Attendant."

So the other day, the boss calls me in when I was on a break. You might ask what does a men's-room attendant do when *he* takes a break? The same thing that anyone else does: go to the bathroom, have a cigarette, sit down. That sort of thing. So the boss says to me, "We're going 'All Gender.' You are now an All Gender bathroom attendant." I was stunned. But then I thought, hey, as long as they wash their hands, hell, I'll be an "All *Species*" bathroom attendant if that'll keep my job.

So, immediately, the boss changes the name on the door to "All Gender" and puts up new bathroom symbols as well. Instead of just a cutout of a man, he puts up a cutout of a man, next to a cutout of a woman, next to a cutout of a man with half a dress on. *Why'd he even stop there?* I think.

So, first night on the job, no problem. Guy comes in. Bim-boom-bang. Faucets, towel, tip—no problem. The guy probably couldn't read. What does he know?

Then the "All Gender" kicks in, big-time. A lady comes in. She says, "What're *you* doing here?" I say, "This is where I work. I'm taking care of things." She says, "Well, that doesn't include me. Get out." So I say, "What're you, firing me? This is my job." We have this argument. Now, remember, I'm a college graduate (Haverford '68. Haverford's very progressive. The president there worked as a garbage man in his spare time, I think.) I stand my ground. If it'd been Florida and I'd had a gun, I would've pulled it.

When I don't move—remember, always polite, that's the most important part of the job—the lady goes into a stall, not happy with the situation at all. To tell you the truth, I find that "All Genders" are, generally, very unhappy people. She comes out. I run the water. She looks at me like I'm registered in the neighborhood and leaves. Doesn't even check her hair. OK, so I saved on the towel.

Sometimes when I run the water, the guy will tell me, "Too late. Don't need it. I already went." Everybody's a comedian.

Next is an old man. Tells me he's a Vietnam vet. Lost the use of his arms in the war. He needs help. I look at the guy long and hard. Maybe if I was a kid I'd fall for something like that. Like it was a school bet or something. But he stands there with his arms at his side. "I need help," he says. "Vietnam." Like that's supposed to say it all. Which it does, I guess. So I say, "*I* was in 'Nam." How many klicks from Da Nang to Khe Sanh?" "About 335," he says. "But you can't go there straight or Charlie will get you. As the

Huey flies, it's maybe 250 klicks. By F-4, it's thirty seconds." I figure he's telling the truth. He was in country. So I help him. Nice guy. Gave me ten bucks. Then I think, hey, at that rate, if this guy's drinkin' beer in some hooch all night, it could get expensive. After I zip him up, I say, "Semper fi, buddy," and he says, "Huh?" He doesn't know what I'm talking about. I go, "Hoooooraaaaaagh," and he says, "Faggot," and leaves. Now, I *know* he was faking because, to tell you the truth, he looked like he coulda masturbated anytime he wanted to if he really put his mind to it. Both hands. The guy was a complete faker *and* an "All Gender."

When the boss first said "All Gender," I thought he'd said, "All *Jenner*." Like I used to think "transgender" and transjenner" were the same thing. Then I came to learn that "transjenner" means you still got your cock and balls. That's "transgender lite." That's when I thought, hey, maybe I'll meet an Olympic champ. Or at least a Kardashian.

Anyway, next was two teenage girls. They thought it was hysterical—me being in there with the towels. They were more worried about what I'd *hear* than what I'd see. Talk, talk, talk. Lotta mirror action. Finally, they flush and go like I wasn't even there. That's the thing about "All Genders": lousy tippers.

Actually, the job is very much like the way Milton put it in his "On His Blindness" poem (I *told* you I was a college graduate. Haverford '68). "They also serve who only stand and wait." That's me. Standing and waiting. "For what?" I ask myself. Towels, soap, and smells. That's what. When I hear people say, "Business is picking up," I think, you don't *know* picking up like I know picking up. *Garbage* men get better smells on the job than I do. Yeah, that's it. I'm a sanitation worker, basically. But I'm on the *front lines* of sanitation, if you know what I mean. I get it when it first comes out, so to speak.

I knew an Elvis impersonator men's-room attendant in Vegas. He did what I do only he did it at Caesar's and in costume. He was somewhere between a "Comeback Elvis" and the one with the jumpsuits and sequins. But it was weird having the King in there. Even for me. I didn't get into it with him. I acted like a civilian.

So lemme clear a few things up here. Maybe put a little air freshener on the subject. Men's-room attendants broke the color line long before *Brown v. Board of Education*. We were "All Races" long before we were "All Gender." So now, I guess, we're breaking the gender line. Next, maybe I'll be replaced by a smartphone and a towel dispenser or something. Or maybe there'll even be some sort of "green screen" in there so people can pretend they're pissing at the Taj Mahal.

But right now I'm learning to adapt. The "All Gender" thing doesn't bother me because if there's one thing I've learned in this business, it's that we're all the same— sort of. Well, not really, of course, but that's the way you have to act if you're going to do a turn as an "All Gender" bathroom attendant. That's why I always say to myself, no matter what: "Hey, we're all the same." And then I say to myself, but very secretly so nobody can hear me, "What the Fuck?????"

WRITE WHAT YOU EMOJI

- I'm feeling very happy right now, right here, at the end of this sentence.

- That makes me feel kinda sad, I guess, but not *that* sad. Not like "death" sad. More like end-of-a-good-movie sad. Or the sad you feel when something good ends. Like a TV series you're binge watching, and the weekend's not over yet. Or sex. Yeah, that's it. It's mainly like sex. Forget everything I said before. I'm feeling as if we just had sex, and it's over. I mean, the sex and the relationship. OK? It's not you, it's…No, wait a minute. Lemme make this real clear. It *is* you. That's how I feel right now. It's definitely not me that's making me sad.

- It was a *joke*, get it? You know, like, *funny*? At least, I *think* it's funny. Not the funniest, mind you. But still, pretty goddamn funny. It's all subjective, I guess, but I'm talkin' funny ha-ha, not funny weird. Just funny. Sort of. Oh well, I tried. I *thought* it was funny.

- That last sentence was pretty foolish. You know, like sweat drops all over the place and my tongue hanging out like Miley-Cyrus-on-steroids foolish. I feel really stupid right now. I wish I had *two* tongues to hang out. *That's* how foolish I feel. OK?

- I'm winking. And it isn't a tic or anything. It's a wink. Like, an "I know that you know that I know that you know" sorta thing.

- In the silent-movie days, they'd called what I'm trying to say a "doh," or to *really* make the point, a "double-doh." That's when one of the Little Rascals would look right into the camera and make a Buckwheat face like someone just stuck something up his ass, and he isn't sure if he liked it or not. "Double doh," dude. Get it? I don't know what to make of the whole thing except my mouth, right now, looks like a black hole.

- My whole life is clumping. You ever clean out a litter box? You know, with all the clumps? That's me right now. All clumped and not happy about it. I look beat up and, let's face it, clumpy as hell. Not only that, I smell like cat piss. Why doesn't someone clean up after *me,* for a change? Like with a strainer scoop? I'm entitled. And how 'bout some fresh litter once in a while? Maybe even "World's Best." OK?

- I laughed so hard I peed in my pants, but those drops are "laugh sweat," not pee. The urination is off-screen. It was so funny I thought I'd die. But in a funny way. Like falling into a vat of softener. That would be listed as an industrial accident by OSHA, but it would *still* be funny. How did your husband die? It was at work. He slipped and fell into an open vat of…softener, but they couldn't get him out in time. Wha? Humor is always double-edged. But this was fun-ny.

- My mother used to say, "I'm so mad I could spit." That's how I feel right now. I could spit. Of course, nowadays, she'd probably say something much dirtier. But I didn't want to get into that, emoji-wise. But I *am* angry, get it? If you could see me right now you'd be like Robert Young in those old coffee commercials. You'd say, "Hey, Jim, why so tense?" But when I told you, you'd nod and say, "Well, you got a point there." See? I don't have to apologize for being mad. It's appropriate. But the emoji means nobody's going to get hurt. I'm just mad as hell.

- Those aren't tears of joy. They're tears of "I want you to like me but not more than I like you." OK? I mean, it's very important that I come across as an OK person who can roll with the punch. But don't punch me. I don't like that. I mean, I want to be a good egg (I'm an <u>ovo</u>-vegetarian, by the way.) I want to make a point, but I don't want to be strident. I wink a lot when I talk—like, sometimes, every word. And I use air quotes, too, so nobody gets the wrong idea.

- Hey, hey, hey. Back off. I didn't mean it *literally*. Only as a *possibility. Maybe.* OK? There's enough trouble in the world without people getting all "Trumpy" on one another. Chill. Take a chill pill. Take a chill *enema*, for all I care. Or put yourself on a chill drip. Just be cool and relax. Nobody's challenging you, OK? OK, I *am* challenging you *slightly*, but only your intellect. Not bodily. "No readers were injured in this sentence." But I do take exception, which is just this side of acceptance. Just a thought. OK? Friends?

- You racist bastard. Emoji are *not* Chinese. Go fuck yourself. The squinty thing is bliss, not Asian. And the next thing you know, you'll start calling the sun Chinese, too, because it's the same color as Mao Zedong. Who are you, Hitler?

- Yep, that's how I feel. If you want to call it "smug," then smug I am. Smug R Us. Smugamemnon. All of it. Pleased as punch. I like it, and I like me.

- It's not as simple as that. Nothing is. It's complicated as the devil. Like a sideways waffle in economics. I'm happy/sad for you. The way God is. Nothing personal. I just don't feel anything, really. But I'm not numb, because I *do* feel that I'm not feeling. I'm blinking. Rapidly. And also squinting and winking. I know it looks crazy. Crazy and clear at the same time. Sorta like I get the whole suicide-bombing thing now. Someone says, "You wanna be a suicide bomber?" And I say, "Sure," because I think he'll like me. But then, how can he like me if I'm not going to be around? Or if I *am* around to take advantage of agreeing to be a suicide bomber, how long will I still get the "liking" part before he says, "Hey, I thought you were going to do it. You're an asshole." Then I've really blown it with him, and maybe I *will* blow myself up just to show him and make him like me after all. But then what? That's how I feel…like a needy suicide bomber who has to constantly be told she's desirable. It's a no-win situation, especially if you're not good with people or a joiner. Let's face it. Basically, no one wants a suicide bomber around even if it makes them like you at first for saying you'll do it. That's how I feel.

MEMORIES OF THE EL NIÑO WINTER OF GLOBAL WARMING

- Air-conditioning subsidies for the poor
- Santa in his sleighmobile
- No two raindrops alike
- Draining the walk after a big storm
- Downhill slipping

Everything's Wront

- Water hockey

- Oilskin scarves

- Rubber as a *really* fake fur

- Northern neon lights

- "I'm Dreaming of a Dry Christmas"

- "Chestnuts Drying on an Open Fire"

- 33 (Chilean miners) Below

- Rain, dear

- Putting up the Christmas umbrella

- The Iditarod Chihuahua race

- Cinqo de Janayo

- North Pole dancing

- Canada—"C'mon on Up"

- Jack Frost slurping at your toes

- Water ski bunnies

- Cross-country galoshing

- School "flood days"

A STATEMENT FROM CHARLIE SHEEN'S PENIS

I HAD NOTHING TO DO WITH IT! Don't look at me. I only do what I'm told. I'm *blind*, for crissakes. My one so-called eye is really a mouth, you know, in case you haven't noticed. I don't want to say I was only following orders, but it's *true*. Without Charlie leading the way, I'm lost. I wouldn't even know where to go, you know what I mean? Even the urination thing wasn't up to me. It was all him. *He* decided. And believe me, sometimes he *didn't* decide—at least not in the old days. And the next thing you knew, I was swimming in a world of wet in the middle of his pants.

I wish I had a nickel for every time I slept in piss. Maybe I'd be able to buy my way out of this situation.

So now, Charlie's HIV. What does this *mean?* Not for him, for *me.* I used to be the most famous penis in Hollywood. Right up there with Forrest Tucker, Roddy McDowall, and Uncle Miltie—but not for size, for the activity. I was the original action hero: always ready, always agreeable, and always happy. A "stand up" guy. That was me. Do I have to say, "*Winning?*" Now it's more like "*Whining!*" I don't even like to go to the bathroom now. People are afraid of me. *Me!* Can you believe it? The most lovable thing in Hollywood. Now I got little purple bruises all over me. Not from the HIV—take it easy. The little purple circles are from people touching me with a ten-foot pole, and most of them don't even want to do *that*. That's no life for a penis. I should be out and about—standing up, happy, and proud. You know what I mean: "Hello, world, here I am." But no! Now, Charlie's HIV. So what exactly does that make me? Typhoid Harry? Hey, don't kill the messenger. I had nothing to do with it. You think a penis has a brain *or* a conscience? No! I got neither. Never had. It was always just me.

Oh, the places I've been. The things I've see. Don't ask. Charlie was an equal-opportunity lover, you know, but I was never an equal-opportunity prick. I had my own likes and dislikes, and I wasn't afraid to express them. When I didn't like something, I would just take myself out of the fray, lie down, and go to sleep.

So what now? you ask. What does the most active penis in Hollywood do when the guy he's attached to is HIV? Go into retirement? Go back to pissing my life away like I did when I was ten? Hey, I've got my whole life ahead of me. I may be retired, but I'm not dead. I've seen those retirement ads. This could be the most rewarding time of my life. The "sunset years." Maybe you'll see me lying around on the beach or hanging out at the golf course. I may be down, but I'm not out by any means. I'll be fine. I may *look* depressed and all hangdog, but I'm not. I'm fine. Just as long as Charlie doesn't do one thing: go the reassignment route. I may be a little prick, but I'm no Bruce Jenner. And I am also four square against plastic surgery. I plan to age gracefully—wrinkles and droopy balls and all. So, I'll see you around. No, I won't. What am I saying? I take that back. I'm blind, remember? But call me if they find a cure.

OVERHEARD AT THE ST. PATRICK'S DAY PARADE

- "Is that the Wearin' o' the Green? Or did you just throw up on your shirt?"

- "Erin go Bragh, baby." It means if you're Irish, you better be topless. Erin go *bra*.

- "Is that your wife or just Paddy's Pig?" Oh well, "Any pork in a storm," as they say.

- "Tis the longest failed sobriety test in the world."

- "Kiss me. I'm Irish." The only way to make sense of that is if it were a felony as well.

- "Irish homosexuals are marching again this year." Which gives new meaning to the term *Gaelic*. But then again, I guess, there's a little lavender in *all* the Irish.

- "Grand marshal of the St. Patrick's Day Parade isn't like being captain of the Titanic…it's like being one of the passengers."

- "This crowd looks like a Rudolph the Red-Nosed Reindeer convention."

- "Is that a leprechaun, or just Bob Costas in a sweater?"

HOW YOU KNOW YOU WERE BORN BEFORE 1996

- The other day you yelled "Asshole" at a driverless car.

- You still think Facebook has something to do with freshmen girls.

- You asked your dry cleaner to "Spotify" a couple of your ties.

- You were completely devastated when you found out your blind date just got out of jail.

Everything's Wront

- You think "Eat local" is a come-on.

- "Beats" are hippies not earphones.

- You're glad Bill Gates finally fixed his hair.

- "Larry the Cable Guy" is exactly like your cable guy.

- Your thumb is still only used for the space bar.

- "The Weekend" is for relaxing not rapping.

ALTERNATIVE ACADEMY AWARDS TRIBUTE MONTAGES

- Dead-career montage.
- Dead-to-*you m*ontage.
- Expired leases in Malibu Colony.
- Lose-my-number montage.
- Faces that haven't moved since 2003.

Everything's Wront

- People who like to get their picture taken too much.

- Actors who appear lost when you see them at a stoplight.

- Failed marriages.

- Divorces where the other woman was the nanny.

- Formerly heterosexual.

- Formerly anything.

- Gay unless you publish it.

- Arrogantly bi.

- Women who've kissed Charlie Sheen.

- Men who've kissed Charlie Sheen who thought it was just part of the orgy.

- Writers who thought the actors on a movie set would always be their friends.

- Lawyers we wish were dead.

- Keith Richards—too soon?

- Agents making more money off an estate than when those clients were alive.

- Abandoned cars on the PCH.

- Celebrities who spoke at more than five funerals last year.

- Comedians who bombed (died) on their HBO specials.

- Celebrities who should have declined a Jimmy Fallon on-air parlor game.

- Newscasters who ended up on *Funny or Die*.

- Actors doing reverse-mortgage ads.

- Movies that didn't open.

- Career suicides.

- Audience members when a comedian "killed."

- Jeb Bush supporters.

- Dick Cheney impersonators.

- Singers on cruise ships.

- Oscar hosts who are never asked back.

- Actresses who show up for auditions in costume.

- Writers in development.

- Larry King on a good day.

MY DICTIONARY BY DONALD TRUMP

Ballot (n.) Huge chance for some fantastic signage—e.g., "The Trump Ballot."

Bankrupt (n.) 1. Some people are bankrupt. *I'm* not bankrupt.
Have I ever been bankrupt? People have *gone* bankrupt trying to make me go bankrupt. But I have never, personally, been bankrupt. 2. Financial term meaning "partner."

Barber (n.) Magician. Highest paid member of my staff.

Basic (adj.) Everything I know. Basically, I have a pretty basic knowledge of a lot of basic things. Basically, it's that simple.

Birth (v.) No problem, as long as it takes place in America. Otherwise, who's the mother? Do you know who the mother is? *I* don't know who the mother is. *Somebody's* the mother. Obama and Cruz were anchor babies, but not for this country.

Bombastic (n.) Normal, everyday speech.

Border (n.) Property line, wall footing.

Congress (n.) Losers.

Election (n.) A means by which millions of people get to choose me.

Everyone (n.) Some guy I pay for research.

Fantastic (adj.) Looks good, smells bad.

Fox (n.) 1. Wily, doglike animal known for intelligence and guile. 2. A very good-looking woman. 3. Conservative news outlet known for its blonde anchors—e.g., Megyn Kelly. Been there, wooed her.

Germs (n.) Worse than ISIS. The real threat.

Great (adj.) 1. Term used to describe me. 2. Did I say I was great? 3. Oh yeah, right. *See* "Like America *used* to be."

Hair (n.) A man's best friend. Better than a fourth wife. Hair is definitely a "10."

Huge (adj.) Anything bigger than my mouth—e.g., losses incurred by others while doing business with me.

Immigrant (n.) Campaign issue. *See* "Leaf blower."

Iowa (n.) State in the Midwest that starts with an *I*, so it must have something to do with me.

ISIS (n.) Huge supporters. Without them, nobody would listen to me.

Lightweight (n.) Half a man—a "Trimp."

Look (v.) Imperative verb meaning "Pay attention to what I'm about to say because I'm going to insult you."

Loser (n.) Anyone who's not me—an "un-Trump."

Lot (n.) Much more than you have right now. In fact, a *lot* more.

Golf (n.) 1. Good excuse for carrying a club ("Speak loudly and carry a thin stick.") 2. Justification for environmental devastation. 3. Tricky way of limiting land use to only a few people who have actually paid me money.

Melania (n.) Chronic mental disorder characterized by thinking one's wife is the greatest beauty in the world, and way better than Heidi Klum or Megyn Kelly combined.

Money (n.) Better unit of measurement than inches.

Poll (n.) 1. The only number that counts. 2. The thing in my pants. 3. What I wouldn't touch Rosie O'Donnell with even if it was a *twenty*-foot one.

pout (n.) (v.) 1. My bitchy resting face. Holding the mouth in such a way as to resemble the act of kissing the mirror I'm standing in front of. 2. A silent way of saying, "I'm fantastic, and everyone knows it." *See* "Facial anus."

President (n.) I accept, but "Trump" has to come first. After the election, it should be "Trump President," not the other way around.

Primary (n.) 1. The main thing. It must have something to do with me. 2. A local election to ratify me.

Rosie O'Donnell (n.) Monster, an animal.

Schlonged (v., past tense) Beaten down and made to lie flat; totally collapsed and unnaturally folded over; lifeless, limp; appearing foolish and fake; an object of ridicule and disdain. *See* "Does this hair make me look fatuous?"

Sex (n.) Marriage proposal.

Size (n.) Always measured in penises, not fingers.

Trouble (n.) What everyone else is in except Donald Trump.

Voters (n.) Suckers. They'll buy anything.

White House (n.) Let's face it. A so-so guest cottage in Washington. Not luxurious at all. I bet the roof leaks. When I'm president, maybe *that's* where the wall should go.

NEW MARIJUANA-RELATED PRODUCTS

- "Groovy Feast Cat Food"—Genuine free-range mouse meat with marijuana added. Know why your cat purrs.

- "The Canni-bus"—Public buses that run exclusively on marijuana. "Hey, good fumes, man!"

- Mary Janes"—Little girls' dress shoes made with "potten" leather. Catholic boys looking down at them are too stoned to see reflections.

- "Pot Holders"—Oven mitts *and* tweezers in one.

- "Weed Whacker"—A fly swatter for extinguishing joints dropped in dangerous places.

- "Irrational Joy Dishwashing Liquid"—Liquid soap with marijuana. "Can't get past the swirl, man."

- "100 Percent Marijuana Yule Log"—Endless televised loop of a burning log made entirely of marijuana. "I swear I'm getting high just looking at it."

- "El Chapo Stick"—Marijuana lip balm.

- "Stunnades"—Marijuana-laced appetite suppressants. "You still get the munchies, but nothing looks good."

- "Pot-Sticker Dumplings"—A magical mixture of marijuana and Crazy Glue.

- "Ben-LBGT Pain-Relieving Cream"—Cannabis pain ointment that makes you question your joints and be ambivalent about the pain.

- "GPS Chocolate Chip Cookies"—Cookies with marijuana and a GPS ("Goodie Positioning System") device baked inside. When you drop one in your lap, you don't have to wait till you're straight to find it.

- "Marijuana-Fueled Driverless Car"—Not only driverless, but aimless, too (recommended for the DEA).

- "Joint Chiefs"—The newest NFL franchise.

- "Sub-Zero Reeferidgerator"—*Very* cool.

- "Ten-Foot Selfie Stick"—No more telltale red-eye on Facebook.

- "Ping Bong"—Two paddles, one net, no ball.

- "Budzweizer"—Marijuana-flavored beer. "For all you haven't done, these Budz for you."

IF MARIJUANA HAD BEEN LEGAL IN THE '60S AND '70S

- **Walter Cronkite:** "And that's the way it is…You see, it *is*, and yet, it also *isn't* that way or *any* way. Get it? Heavy."

- **Honeymooners:** "Alice, one of these days…One of these days…Um, *where* is it I always say I'm gonna send you?"

- **Ben Casey:** "Come on, it's not brain surgery. I can't believe I just said that. Are you laughing? *I'm* a brain surgeon, right? I mean, that is *so* funny."

- **Ping Pong:** "Two paddles, one net, no ball. Ping *Bong*, man."

- **CHiPs:** "Doritos! Right now!"

- **Star Wars:** "May the shit be with you. You got any?"

- **I Love Lucy:** "Lucy, you got some 'splainin' to do." "Oh, Ricky, you are so right. I am *really* fucked up."

- **All in the Family:** "Why do you call me that, Arch? I don't smoke meat.

- **Moon Landing:** "One small toke for man, one giant bogart for mankind."

- **Martin Luther King:** "I have a dream. It is so cool. Outasight!"

- **NASA:** "Whitney, we have a delivery."

PRESIDENT DONALD J. TRUMP—THE FIRST 100 DAYS

- First Lady now referred to as "First Piece of Ass."

- Disney forced to retire Donald Duck.

- Oval Office made square because it reminds the president too much of Chris Christie.

- Washington, "D.T.," not "D.C."

- "Hump Day" becomes "Trump Day.

- Strategic Air Command now "Fantastic Air Command."

- NFL forced to have a Super Bowl *every* Sunday.

- Department of Health and Human Services renamed "Department of Losers."

- Supreme Court now just the "Above-Average Court."

- All maps required to designate upstate New York as the "Extra Long and Slender Finger Lakes Region."

- House Ways and Means Committee becomes the "House No Way and Very Mean Committee."

- The White House now "Trump House."

- All door knockers in Washington augmented with silicon.

- Grand Tetons now the "Yuuuuuuge Tetons."

- Camp David now Camp Donald.

- Mar-a-Lago decorator appointed Secretary of the Interior.

- Environmental Protection Agency is merged with Health and Human Services and becomes the "Department of Purell."

- Vice president renamed "loser low-energy president."

- POTUS now "POTRUMP."

- Skin cancer no longer called Melanoma out of respect for First Lady

- Germs replace ISIS as the number one enemy.

- Megyn Kelly put on a no-fly list.

- Golf replaces baseball as the national pastime.

- "USS" designation for War Ships replaced with "Trump". It's the "Trump Intrepid", "Trump George Washington", etc. now.

- Field commanders ordered to say, "You're fired" instead of just "Fire!"

- Supreme Court justices are chosen via a special edition of *Celebrity Apprentice.*

- The Rose Garden is renamed "Trump Garden Place."

- Washington Monument becomes the "Trump Finger Tower."

- "Jeb" is the new name for a drone.

- All official planes except "Air Force One" are called "Air Force Losers."

- Air Force One upgraded to Air Force Ten

- Marine One helicopter grounded because of excessive windage when transporting President Trump.

- "Secretary of Hair" becomes a cabinet position.

- "UST" not "USA."

- President declares a National Day of Hair.

- Civil-rights advocates sing, "We Shall Over Comb."

- Thanksgiving pardon of national turkey is replaced by apology to Carly Fiorina.

- DEFCON 5 declared if Rosie O'Donnell enters the Beltway.

- Closes down Federal Reserve; opens Trump Federal Casino.

- Seal Team 6 works security for all press conferences.

- "State of the Union" replaced with "State of the Ego."

- Neutralizes Putin by sending Christie to stand behind him whenever he appears in public.

- Rejects gun control in favor of much stricter comb control.

- First president to wear a baseball cap for his official portrait.

- Replaces White House fence with a wall. Mexico gladly foots the bill.

- Signs his first bill and is amazed it didn't cost him anything.

- Begins plans for Trump Presidential Library to house *The Art of the Deal.*

- Invades Rosie O'Donnell.

- Finally realizes the *Situation* Room has nothing to do with the *Jersey Shore.*

- Finally adjusts to living in a smaller house.

- Tells the Navy guy carrying "the football", "You're fired!" North Korea is immediately destroyed.

Everything's Wront

- United States files for bankruptcy—but not the president, personally.

- Yells, "Get him out!" at a protester in San Francisco. Two thousand people are immediately identified as homosexual.

- Tries to get his portrait on the twenty-dollar bill, but the engraver says his hair looks too engraved.

- Shocked when he finds out the Lincoln Bedroom is not named after a car.

- Finally stops referring to the White House as the "clubhouse."

- Every time he hears "The Star-Spangled Banner," he can't help thinking about Marla Maples in hot pants.

- Cancels the Easter Egg Roll because he wants to prove he's pro-life.

- Gets face measured for Mount Rushmore.

- Changes the name of the White House to the "White-a-lago."

- Orders golf carts to Afghanistan instead of Humvees.

- Celebrates Chinese New Year with a parade on Pennsylvania Avenue featuring a papier-mâché Rosie O'Donnell and firecrackers.

- Redecorates the Lincoln Memorial with chandeliers.

- Asks Congress to approve a Trump golf course on The Mall.

- New Motto: "In Trump We Trust."

- Nominates Stevie Wonder to administer his blind trust.

- "Hail to the Donald" replaces "Hail to the Chief".

- Pardons Hillary Clinton.

IF POLITICAL-CAMPAIGN SLOGANEERS WROTE HEADLINES FOR E.D. MEDICATION ADS

- Keep Erections Alive
- Ask Not What Your Erection Can Do for You; Ask What You Can Do for Your Erection
- We Have Nothing to Fear but Erectile Dysfunction Itself
- I Like Erections
- We Want Erections

- Make Erections Great Again
- Tippecanoe And Erections, Too
- Are Your Erections Better Off Than They Were Four Years Ago?
- The Audacity of Erections
- Yes We Can Keep an Erection
- A Thousand Points of Erections
- Time for an Erection
- Four More Erections
- Heal, Engorge, Revive
- It's the Erections, Stupid
- Right to Rise
- New Possibilities, Real Erections
- An Erectile Revolution Is Coming
- Reigniting the Erections of America
- From Hope to Higher Erections
- Defeat the Washington Erectile Dysfunction; Unleash the American Erection
- It's Morning Erections Again in America
- Don't Swap Erections in the Middle of a Stream
- Happy Erections Are Here Again
- Erections We Can Believe In
- All the Way with BJ
- Yes, We Can Get an Erection
- A New American Erection
- Hillary for Erections
- From Hope to Higher Erections
- Rebuild the American Erection

- Restore the American Dream for Hardworking Erections
- An Erection You Can Believe In
- Erections You Can Trust
- Ready to Have an Erection on Day One
- Erections for Us
- Reform. Growth. Erection.
- America Needs an Erection
- Let's Get Erections Moving Again
- A New Erection for a New America
- America's Top Erection
- The Better Erection for a Better America
- An Erection Called Hope
- Time for an Erection
- Building an Erection to the Future
- Moving Erections Forward
- An Erection for the New Millennium
- Give 'em Erections, Harry
- Grant Us Another Erection
- An Erection in Every Pot
- Erection Days Are Here Again
- Life, Liberty, and Erections
- We Want Erections
- Win with Erections
- I'm Just Wild about Erections
- Peace and Erections
- We Can Do Erections
- In Your Erection, You Know He's Right

- The Erection's the One
- To Begin a New Erection
- Erections: Now More Than Ever
- A Leader, for An Erection
- Where's the Erection?
- Kinder, Gentler Erections
- Erections for a Change
- It's Erections to Change America
- Putting Erections First
- Compassionate Erections
- A Stronger Erection
- Let Erections Be Erections Again
- Yes We Can Have Erections
- Erections First
- Reform, Prosperity, and Erections
- Believe in Erections
- Restore Erections Now
- Erections Aren't Working
- An Erection to Believe In
- Feel the Erection
- Erections For America
- I'm with Erections
- A New American Erection
- Courageous Erections
- Erections Can Fix It
- From Erections to Higher Ground
- The Better Man for a Better Erection

OSCAR ACCEPTANCE-SPEECH MISTAKES

- I really wanted to thank all the little people…but, unfortunately, we didn't make *The Wizard of Oz*.

- Holding this statue like this feels like something very familiar.

- Mom, if you're up there….Why are you working as a stagehand?

- It's an honor just to have *had* liposuction.

- I want to thank God for this…So I guess this means killing that guy was OK, right?

- And to my wife…Get ready for some Oscar Meyer tonight, baby.

- Is it me, or is this thing vibrating? Oh, look, batteries!

- Accepting this award on behalf of me, is *me*.

- Who posed for this thing: Al Gore or Mitt Romney?

- This statue doesn't have any genitals…This isn't an Oscar, it's a gold-plated Ken Doll.

- The other nominees are a bunch of untalented skinny bitches.

- Wow! That casting couch really worked.

- I learned so much from our director. Like, there's no *n* in "Cut"!

- There are so many people to thank. Just like an orgy.

- You *like* me, you *really* liked my $2 million Oscar campaign.

UNUSUAL FILM CREDITS

- Bulimia Coach to Ms. Hemmings

- Zit Wrangler

- Stunt Double Double

- Craft Services Taster

- Thanks to Woodlawn Cemetery for Prostheses and Props

- Water-Retention Surrogate for Ms. Hemmings

- Well-above-Average Boy

- Unit Fluffer

- Female Extra Puller for Mr. Kane

- "Cut" Man

- "You're Welcome"—God

- Lip Service Provided by Collagen R Us

- For Information on What Those Guys Do Who Seem to Just Stand Around, Call 310-555-9820

INDICATIONS THAT YOUR VALENTINE HATES YOU

- He asks you to shave his back during sex.

- He gives you a box of chocolates, but he hides your insulin.

- The string of pearls he promised turns out to be two dozen unopened oysters.

- When she sleeps with her mouth open, there's a sign that says, "Men Working."

- When you tell her you want to give her a piano, she says, "I only like the black keys."

- When he invites you out for a Valentine's Day dinner, he asks if you can carry a tray.

- She puts a picture of Osama Bin Laden in the locket you gave her.

- The vows she wants to renew are the ones about never wanting to see you again as long as she lives.

- The lingerie he gives you is in *his* size.

- Penicillin instead of perfume.

- The Valentine he gave you had "Merry Christmas" crossed out...and a picture of somebody else's kids.

- She says the heart-shaped box of candy you sent her looks like a toilet seat.

STEPHEN HAWKING'S PICKUP LINES

1) Hey, baby, how 'bout some computer-generated oral sex?

2) How'd you like to have my voice synthesizer go down on you?

3) Kiss me. I feel a computer-generated pucker coming on.

4) The last time I had a hard-on, I married it.

5) Am I turned on by you, or is that just drool on my pants?

6) Ever gotten good head from a real genius?

7) I can't move, I can't speak, and I can't eat. But my mind is a great fuck.

8) Don't worry. I won't cum in you. My dick is on "Pause."

9) Wanna see if I can hack into your pussy?

10) I'd ask you to sit on my face, but somebody already did.

11) If you've never felt the earth move, I have a formula for that.

12) I control my penis with my cheek. If you kiss me there, it's like getting my cock sucked.

13) When I cum, I have to type "Oh, God!"

14) I have a speech impediment. It's called my mouth.

15) I'm the only guy you'll ever meet who has a wheelchair for his cock.

16) If I told you I could be cured by being fucked, would you at least think about it?

"OCTOBER SURPRISES" WE KINDA SAW COMING

- Ivanka Trump, a recent convert to Judaism, decides to out-Malia Malia and take a JAP year.

- General Petraeus invades another mistress.

- Hillary Clinton wears a skirt.

- Larry David mounts a third-party candidacy.

- Gwyneth Paltrow gets treated for Goop.

- Beyonce's extensions get their own record deal.

- Donald Trump announces his hair is pregnant and gives birth to a 7.7-pound toupee. Donald is identified as the father. Apparently, he finally did what people have been telling him to do for years.

- Schwarzenegger's love child marries a Kennedy.

- A Kardashian enters a "for profit" college but leaves when she doesn't get paid.

- The "DTs" are reclassified as an election-year-only disorder.

- The NFL investigation into concussions is expanded to cover domestic partners.

- Somebody kills Bill O'Reilly.

- Chris Christie removes the traffic cones that were placed across his small intestines by a trusted aide.

- *Hamilton* tickets are no longer scalped. They're "hedge funded."

- Bill Clinton has another bypass. This time he says no to a Westchester MILF.

- Bill Cosby launches a one-man show that is immediately considered the first suicide bombing by an American.

- The Academy announces that, next year, the Oscar statue will have cornrows.

- Charlie Sheen admits his version of "streaming" has nothing to do with television.

- Caitlyn Jenner gets hired as a ball girl for the U.S. Open.

- Kim Jong-un finally fires his barber.

- China establishes takeout on the disputed islands in the South China Sea.

- Jeb Bush demands a recount.

- Vice President Joe Biden announces there's nothing wrong with presidential implants.

- Rick Perry finally remembers that third thing he would have eliminated.

- Justin Trudeau vows to build a wall around Barbra Streisand.

- The Electoral College disavows Trump University.

- David Cameron starts referring to the EU as the "Eeeeeyuuuuu!"

- Bo, the unarmed presidential dog, is shot by a white D.C. police officer.

TEN JOKES USING THE COMIC TROPE OF THE JAPANESE MISPRONUNCIATION OF THE WORD *ERECTION*

- For Donald Trump, this biggest election of his life. He act like he never have election before.

- This good election day. I take many Viagra this morning.

- I love election. It give me chance to spend time with wife in small booth with drawn curtain.

- Why always talk about rigged election? That sick.

- I love election that last more than four hours. Make me feel like Godzirra.

- Once I have four-hour election but only three-hour girlfriend. Must finish election by hand.

- President Clinton highest elected official ever in Oval Office.

- What is difference between *election* and *dictator*? No difference. Both disappear in end.

- E-mail always promise longer election. Why? Long election definition of too much good thing.

- Elections like taxes. Always feel better when someone else do them for you.

- We always lose election with Hillary. Too old and wrinkled.

"MY FAIR MARTY"

THE ROYAL SHAKESPEARE PRODUCTION OF A MUSICAL BASED ON THE LIFE OF MARTIN LUTHER KING

Starring: Benedict Cumberbatch, Bjorn Borg and Gwyneth Paltrow as Coretta Scott King

SONGS:
Why Can't the Negros? ("Learn to Speak!")
Wouldn't It Be Lib'ratin'?
With a Little Bit o' Peaceful Demonstration
I'm a Preacher Kind of Man
Just You March ("Reverend King, Just You March")

Andrew Smith

Poor Reverend King
The Letter to Coretta ("Gets Better in Marietta")
I Could Have Marched all Night
Selma Shuffle
On the Street Where You Sit ("I Have Often Marched Down This Street Before")
Martin's Entrance
The Southern Christian Leadership Gavotte
You Spoke It
Free Me ("Don't Talk of Hate, Don't Make Me Wait, Free Me!")
Get Me to the Jail on Time ("I'm Getting 'rested in the Morning")
A Hymn to Hoover
Without Segregation
I've Grown Accustomed to His Race

SCAMILTON—THE MUSICAL

<u>Lyrics:</u>

BLOOMBERG
How does a bastard, slumlord, son of a bitch and a German,
dropped in the middle of a campaign for president
Ridiculed and spewing so much Muslim hate
Grow up to be the Republican presidential candidate?

TED CRUZ
The $10 billion son of the founding father
Got a lot farther by working a lot harder
By bein' a lot smarter

By bein' a self-starter who liked to hump
By fourteen so they placed him in charge of everything called "Trump"

OBAMA
And every day while immigrants were being deported and carted
Away across the waves, he struggled and kept his guard up
Inside, he was longing for something national to be part of
The brother was ready to beg, steal, barrow, or barter

BERNIE SANDERS
Then 2016 came and devastation reigned
Our man saw his country's future drip, drippin' down the drain
Put a comb to his temple, made his hair look insane
And he wrote his first refrain: *Let Mexico feel the pain.*

BLOOMBERG
Well, word got around, they said, "This guy's insane, man."
Took up donations just to end his presidential claim and
Stop saying you'll send Muslims back from whence they came and
The world's gonna know your name! What's your name, man?

TRUMP
Donald J. Trump, I am
My name's Donald J. Trump, I am
And there's a million things I haven't done
But just you wait, just you wait.

WEIRD DISORDERS IN THE ZOO INFIRMARY

- Cirrhosis of the Beak
- Cranky Carnivore Disease
- Bee's Knees Torn Meniscus
- Tick Tachycardia
- Cockroach Survivor's Guilt
- Canine Toilet Dipsomania
- Walrus Moustache Burn
- Elephant Trunk Viagra Abuse
- Hummingbird OCD
- Bumblebee Asthma
- Anteater Rhinoplasty

- Hammerhead Shark Walleyes
- Moose Rack Envy
- Rabbit Nymphomania
- Dodo Retardation
- Cuckoo-Bird Dementia
- Pathological Lion
- Goose Bumps
- Alligator Psoriasis
- Monkey Shines

RULES TO LIVE BY

- Always share your cookie.

- Assume everyone you meet is having a worse day than you are because, guess what? They are.

- Better late than predictable.

- Do more than you're supposed to.

- The grass is always greener. Period.

- Learn from your dog.

Everything's Wront

- All philosophy is economically derived. Consider the income of anyone who tells you the best things in life are free.

- Never refuse ice cream.

- Act slightly deranged.

- Talk to strangers. If they offer candy, take it.

- Don't say no to a nap.

- Be proud of luck.

- Wear your socks to bed.

- Always carry a pen.

- Never get into a small boat unless you own it.

- Sweat pants.

- Leave all birds alone.

- Never take a radio apart.

- Do what the cop says.

- Brussels sprouts are better than you think.
- When it comes to men's earrings or tattoos, one of either is plenty.
- At barber school you can run with scissors.
- Keys reproduce nonsexually.
- Duct tape fixes everything except a relationship.
- Don't let depression stop you. It just means you're paying attention.
- "Maestro" is a good first name for just about everybody.
- People never want to be accused of "jumping on the bandwagon." It means there's always plenty of room.
- Wear a hat even when you don't have to.
- Deny everything. Shamelessly.
- Always have something in the mail.

DATING TIPS FOR NEWLY DIVORCED MEN

- On your first date with a new woman, never refer to your ex-wife as a "dumb twat". She has one, too.

- Do not refer to your graduation from "Anger Management" as one of the greatest achievements of your life.

- Masturbating while thinking of your first wife is acceptable, but only if you take her picture and put a hole where her mouth used to be.

- Remove the "move out bar" that's still across the back seat of your car. You won't need it until the new woman throws you out.

- Leave the seat up when you urinate at the new woman's house. It will allow her to get her rocks off by thinking she can "civilize" you.

- Refrain from calling the new woman's ex-husband "gay". She'll think it means you think she's a ball buster.

- Avoid wearing anything that the ex-husband forgot to take. Especially his condoms. If she offers you one from the bedside table, say it's too small.

- Always complement a newly-divorced woman's hair. She got it cut and re-styled as a symbol of her new life. Don't make her think it didn't work

- When you call the new woman by the wrong name, tell her it's the patron saint you were praying to that morning.

- Don't try to get friendly with her kids. They hate you and everything about you. The trick is to get into her pants *before* they get into her head about what a loser you are.

Everything's Wront

- If you are dating a newly divorced woman, pay the bartender to "card" her. Especially if she shows up wearing jeans to indicate how young and casual she is instead of the used-up housewife she *knows* she is.

- Don't be afraid if the ex-husband is in jail or has done time. Felons rarely escape, and ex-cons are intimidated by anyone who's not in a hallway house. On the other hand, always take the table in the back facing the door.

- Shoot low. Don't try to date the woman of your dreams. You're not the man of hers. Just remember President Clinton got blowjobs because he always told Monica how thin she looked that day.

- Don't dye your hair. It only works for women and circus ponies. Don't shave our head either. Women dating divorced men assume they're serial killers, or, at the very least, abusers. Try not to prove them right. Which means don't pound the table when you talk, and don't kill them.

- Forget petting. You're not a teenager and neither are her tits.

- Stand far enough away from her, even when your arm's around her, when you're having your picture taken so she can cut you out after you leave. She's knows how to do this.

- Her best friend is hotter than she is. Deal with it. This isn't "The Bachelor".

- Divorced women like slow drivers. They're finished with the "fast lane" and anything that has the word "Go" in it.

- Soap is sexier than cologne. Sleep is sexier than sex. And there's nothing in the men's room that will help.

- You can admit that you don't do shelves.

- Learn to tell your story in three sentences.

BILL CLINTON'S PET PROJECTS AS "FIRST HUBBY"

Just Say What Is, Is
Educational project to teach legal marijuana users how to sound coherent when stoned.

No Intern Left Alone
Program to increase harassment of female government interns.

Intern Beatification Program
Make America adorable again.

Don't Ask
National outreach effort to employ more Jewish Mothers.

The White House Basement Hydroponic Garden
Bill Clinton's commitment to killer leafy greens all year round.

Returning Wife Awareness Project
Setting up an early warning system for family members who come home unexpectedly.

Operation Head...Start!
"They also serve who only kneel and wait."

The Foundation Foundation
Push up bras for needy women in underdeveloped countries.

Blue Dress For Success
White House Initiative to provide stain resistant clothing for unpaid workers.

Re-decorating the White House
King-size waterbed in the Lincoln Bedroom, the new West "Hot" Wing, Cialis Fertilizer in the Rose garden.

Cheating is Fundamental Program
Showing underprivileged and lower income spouses how to get lucky.

The Bill Bill Bill Initiative
Lobbying Congress for legislation that would put the former president's picture on the 20 dollar bill instead of that skank.

Changing Air Force One
C'mon. With two President Clinton's aboard, it deserves to be, at least, "Air Force Ten".

Oval Office Re-Purposing Project
Priority #1: Get the carpet cleaned.

Golf Tee Equality and Same Sex Tee-off Initiative
No more women's tees. They're separate and unequal.

Lip Biting Awareness Campaign
A lower lip is a terrible thing to lose just because you want to be sincere.

The Gennifer Flowers Stamp
Postage stamps are self-adhesive, so you don't have to lick anymore. "I did not put my tongue on that stamp. Not once."

The Saxophone Project
Campaign to make the tenor sax the national horn.

No Furniture Left Behind
Program for renters, lease holders, and migrants that would allow all temporary occupants to take everything with them when the lease is up, or they leave office.

Speak America
An advocacy program to get every American paid anytime he opens his mouth.

Bimbo Relief Fund
Rescue effort to provide desperately needed funds for any discarded friends, neighbors, divorcees, and waitresses now that the wife has her finger on the button.

Re-Registry of Historical Places
National program to remove all those "Bill Clinton Slept Here" plaques.

Chelsea Piers Initiative
Campaign to save Chelsea Piers by re-naming them the Chelsea Clinton Piers.

Save the Endangered Southern Horndog
National effort to rescue the horndog from extinction against a wave of feminism and equal rights.

Servers of America
An offshoot of the Clinton Foundation that seeks to promote personal servers for Secretaries of State from under developed countries.

The Fast Fast Food Project
National campaign to improve pizza delivery time.

Superfluous Husbands Rescue Effort
An international program that seeks to find something meaningful for the husbands of powerful women to do. Started by Denis Thatcher, husband of Margaret. Ulrich Merkel, current chairman.

First Pet Selection Committee
Chairman of a committee to put a dog in the White House who isn't an intern.

MORE DONALD TRUMP PRODUCTS

- **TRUMP LONG JOHNS:** Condoms for men who are Yuuuuuge.

- **TRUMP SUN BLOCK:** Guaranteed to never let you look like an immigrant

- **TRUMP TIRES:** Nothing with the Trump name on it ever goes flat.

- **TRUMPIALIS:** Just the thing for men who can't get it up and be huge.

- TRUMP SHEARS: Scissors that cut both ways.

- TRUMPHONE: If you vote for me, you can call me.

- TRUMPIES: 50 hour energy for after you finish the 5 hour one.

- TRUMPMOBILE: Car that runs completely on hot air.

- TRUMP COMBOVER CLUB FOR MEN: If I can get away with it, you can get away with it.

- TRUMP GPS: The most fantastic product ever for losers. Never be a loser again.

- TRUMP AIR: Not the airline. I sold that. Is there a law against selling? I'm talking Trump *Air*. Air that I have actually breathed. Now you can breathe the same stuff, too and not be such a loser.

- TRUMP VITAMINS: Forget Vitamin A and Vitamin C. This is Vitamin "T". Specially formulated to make you more like me.

- TRUMP IMPLANTS: Let me take you from a miserable Megyn 3 to a fantastic Melania 10.

- BOTRUMPTOX: Inject me into your face so you don't have a "loser resting face"

- TRUMP BRASS KNUCKLES: Just the thing for a nice, peaceful demonstration at a rally.

- TRUMP HAIR COLORING: Blondes have more fun and do better in the polls.

- TRUMP FLAGS: Get one now and avoid the rush. When I'm president, it'll be UST...United States of Trump.

- TRUMP MATTRESSES: Negotiate with style *and* comfort on a Trumpopedic mattress.

- TRUMP WEDDING CHAPELS: If I had one of these available to me, I'd have 10 marriages, not just three.

- TRUMP LIPSTICK: For a pout that won't quit.

- TRUMP OPTICS: See everything *my* way.

- TRUMP, THE COLOGNE: It's the Sweet smell of Excess. For the man who wants to smell like money... a *lot* of money.

- TRUMP GOLD: Why should gold be the most valuable thing? Trump Gold is *better* than gold. Gold is a loser.

- **TRUMP SCREEN DOORS:** The most incredible screen doors you ever saw. The keep mosquitos, flies, gnats, and beetles out. And anyone else you want to keep out, too. Works like a wall. They're fantastic.

- **TRUMP AVACADOS:** Not Mexican in any way, shape, or form. American avocados the way avocados were meant to be. You can rest assured.

- **TRUMP SPEAKERS BUREAU:** Book someone who isn't afraid to tell it like it is. Basically, book me, Donald J. Trump.

- **TRUMP LOW ENERGY PILLS:** I developed these pills myself after debating Jeb Bush. Basically, they're pages of my book, "The Art of the Deal" ground up into little capsules that are a lot easier to take than actually reading it.

- **TRUMP CHICKEN:** Okay, it's not chicken because Donald Trump is not chicken. Got That? And it's not turkey, either, because Trump is not a turkey, either. In fact, I don't have to tell you, or anyone else, what Trump Chicken is or isn't. But, folks, it tastes like chicken. Case closed.

- **TRUMP WONDER BRAS:** You want to be a 10? Who doesn't want to be a 10? Everybody wants to be a 10.

I'm a 10. Wear my bra, and you'll be a 10. Even if you're a guy.

- TRUMP DIVINITY SCHOOL: Why worship a loser like God who does a lot of very bad things. Make no mistake about it. *Very* bad things. At Trump Divinity School, you worship somebody who can actually do something for you. Me!

- TRUMP BASEBALL CAPS: I wear a cap, and you can too. My caps come in only one color: red. Inside, is a special hair revitalizer that conditions your hair for as long as you wear the cap. When you take it off, Voila! Instant swoosh.

- TRUMPURELL ANTISEPTIC GEL: I hate germs. Do you hate germs? Somebody hates germs. I hate germs almost as much as I hate Mexicans. Sometimes, I don't even know the difference. My Trumpurell will kill anything on contact. Especially Cubans.

- TRUMP SWEAT SUITES: I don't seat. Do you sweat? Somebody sweats Trump sweats are "no sweat" sweats. Fantastic. Just the way I like it.

- TRUMP RUNNING SHOES: Talk about a "swoosh"! If you're going to run, you need fantastic running shoes. Trump running shoes are especially made to stomp on protesters and get 'em outa here! Make running Trump again.

- TRUMP WINE: I don't care what year it is. If it's Trump Wine it's a fantastic year. Trump wine is the finest wine ever made. And if you don't believe it, you're drunk… unlike me who has never touched a drop. I don't drink. I just *drive* people to drink.

- TRUMP CHOCOLATES: The finest chocolates anywhere in the world. Dark chocolate, light chocolate, milk chocolate. The Chocolates love me. Did I say Ben Carson endorsed me?

www.ingramcontent.com/pod-product-compliance
Lightning Source LLC
Chambersburg PA
CBHW070138100426
42743CB00013B/2745